Global Brazil and U.S.-Brazil Relations

COUNCIL *on*
FOREIGN
RELATIONS

Independent Task Force Report No. 66

Samuel W. Bodman and
James D. Wolfensohn, *Chairs*
Julia E. Sweig, *Project Director*

Global Brazil and
U.S.-Brazil Relations

Task Force Members

Task Force members are asked to join a consensus signifying that they endorse "the general policy thrust and judgments reached by the group, though not necessarily every finding and recommendation." They participate in the Task Force in their individual, not institutional, capacities.

Jed N. Bailey
Energy Narrative

Samuel W. Bodman

R. Nicholas Burns
*Harvard Kennedy School
of Government*

Louis E. Caldera*
Center for American Progress

Eileen B. Claussen
*Pew Center on
Global Climate Change*

Nelson W. Cunningham*
McLarty Associates

Eli Whitney Debevoise II*
Arnold & Porter LLP

Paula J. Dobriansky*
Thomson Reuters

Shepard L. Forman*
*Center on International
Cooperation*

José A. Fourquet*
DBS Financial Group

Maria C. Freire
*Albert and Mary Lasker
Foundation*

Stanley A. Gacek†
U.S. Department of Labor

Sergio J. Galvis*
Sullivan & Cromwell LLP

Kevin P. Green*
IBM Corporation

Donna J. Hrinak*
PepsiCo, Inc.

*The individual has endorsed the report and signed onto an additional view.

†Gacek participated in the Task Force under his previous affiliation with the American Federation of Labor and Congress of Industrial Organizations. As a current administration official, he has not been asked to join the Task Force consensus.

Contents

Foreword

Brazil has emerged as both a driver of growth in South America and an active force in world politics in the decade since the Council on Foreign Relations (CFR) convened its first Independent Task Force on the country. During this period, Brazil has lifted nearly thirty million of its citizens out of poverty, significantly expanded its middle class, become increasingly active within multilateral institutions and international forums, and weathered the recent worldwide recession—all in a peaceful, market-oriented, and democratic context.

To be sure, Brazil is still contending with important internal concerns—its remaining poor, the growing challenges of climate change, and its ongoing transformation from a commodity-based to an industrial economy, to name just a few. Nevertheless, the message of this report could hardly be clearer: Brazil matters not just regionally but globally. Its decisions and actions will affect the world's economy, environment, and energy future as well as prospects for diplomacy and stability. Brazil is on the short list of countries that will most shape the twenty-first century. U.S and Brazilian foreign policy must adjust accordingly.

This Independent Task Force examines the U.S.-Brazil relationship in light of the considerable developments of the past ten years. It comes at a time when Brazil's new administration, led by President Dilma Rousseff, has had a few months to settle in and chart a course for the country for the next several years. The Task Force recommends that this period be seen as an opportunity for Brazil and the United States to deepen their partnership through expanded governmental and economic ties.

With its growing regional and global role, Brazil will face new responsibilities and expectations. As Brazil seeks to become more active in its region and abroad, some will look to it for guidance and others will expect it to shoulder more burdens on the international stage. The Task

Force recommends that Brazil receive a seat on an expanded United Nations Security Council, in part as recognition of its increased global role, but also to encourage its constructive participation in global affairs.

I would like to thank the Task Force's chairs, Samuel Bodman and James Wolfensohn, for their leadership throughout this project. My thanks extend to all of the Task Force members and observers for contributing their time, significant experience, and expertise to produce a thoughtful report. I also invite readers to review the additional views written by several Task Force members that appear at the end of the report.

This report would not be possible without the supervision of Anya Schmemann, CFR's Task Force Program director, who shepherded this project from beginning to end, and Senior Fellow Julia Sweig, who ably directed this Task Force and oversaw the research and drafting of this report. All have contributed to a substantive and comprehensive document that will help policymakers and others to better understand the reality of Brazil.

Richard N. Haass
President
Council on Foreign Relations
July 2011

Acknowledgments

The report of the Independent Task Force on Brazil is the product of much work and effort by the dedicated members and observers of this Task Force. In particular, I thank our distinguished chairs, Jim Wolfensohn and Sam Bodman, for their leadership and thoughtful direction. It has been a pleasure to work with them.

I am deeply appreciative of the Task Force members' and observers' time and attention and of their invaluable expertise and guidance. Special thanks are owed to Jed Bailey, Michelle Billig Patron, David Rothkopf, and Tanisha Tingle-Smith for their written contributions. João Castro Neves, Luis Cubeddu, Shep Forman, Stan Gacek, Riordan Roett, and David Vegara offered vital assistance during the process as well.

I had the good fortune to travel to Brazil and the region on three occasions for consultations that informed this report. I benefited from briefings by government officials as well as by representatives from the private sector and civil society in Montevideo, Asunción, Brasília, Foz do Iguaçu, Recife, Rio de Janeiro, and São Paulo. The Brazilian foreign ministry, in particular Minister Antonio Patriota and Ambassador Mauro Vieira and their offices, made possible numerous high-level consultations. In addition, thanks go to the many Brazilian officials from a number of ministries who offered their time and insight. Ambassador Thomas Shannon embraced this effort, and, like Ambassador Vieira, briefed the Task Force members and observers in Washington, DC, and graciously hosted a Task Force delegation while we were in Brasília. I owe special thanks to Matias Spektor for his intelligence and guidance throughout this endeavor.

My thanks go to the Brazilian advisory board to the Task Force, whose insights and perspectives greatly enhanced this effort and whose helpful guidance throughout this process paved the way for instructive meetings with representatives of Brazilian civil society in Rio de Janeiro and São Paulo. In particular, my thanks go to Yvonne Bezerra de Mello,

José Pio Borges, Leona Forman, Israel Klabin, Celso Lafer, Luiz Felipe Lampreia, Georges Landau, Maria Regina de Lima, Marcelo Neri, Jair Ribeiro, Carlos Ivan Simonsen Leal, Amaury de Souza, and Ana Toni.

We also received helpful input from many CFR members. The Washington Meetings team organized an event with CFR members in Washington, with Task Force member Riordan Roett and observer Kellie Meiman; the New York Meetings team organized an event for CFR members in New York, led by Task Force members Sergio Galvis and Donna Hrinak; the Corporate Program organized a roundtable in Washington, DC, for executives, led by Task Force member David Rothkopf; and the Outreach Program team organized a session in New York for higher education leaders with Task Force members Shepard Forman and Donna Hrinak.

I extend additional thanks to CFR's Publishing team, which assisted in editing the report and readying it for publication, and CFR's Communications, Meetings, Corporate, External Affairs, and National teams, who all worked to ensure that the report reaches the widest audience possible. My colleagues Laurie Garrett, Michael Levi, Shannon O'Neil, and Jonathan Pearl offered great guidance as well.

Anya Schmemann, along with Kristin Lewis and Shelby Leighton of CFR's Task Force Program, was instrumental to this project from beginning to end. The wisdom, experience, and patience of Anya and her team kept this project on track, while their thoughtful questions and contributions helped to create the strongest possible final product. My research associate Eliza Sweren-Becker deserves the lion's share of the credit and my eternal thanks for her research, drafting, and redrafting of this report. It was my good fortune to benefit from Eliza's commitment, camaraderie, and intelligence from start to finish. I also extend my thanks to Eliza's successor, David Herrero, for seamlessly shepherding the report to final publication.

CFR also expresses its thanks to the Alcoa Foundation for its support for the Global Brazil initiative. Many thanks to CFR President Richard N. Haass and Director of Studies James M. Lindsay, in addition to Janine Hill and Amy Baker, who lent their support to this initiative because they recognize the need for the United States to understand and craft intelligent policies toward Brazil. I hope this effort makes some headway to that end.

Julia E. Sweig
Project Director

Brazil

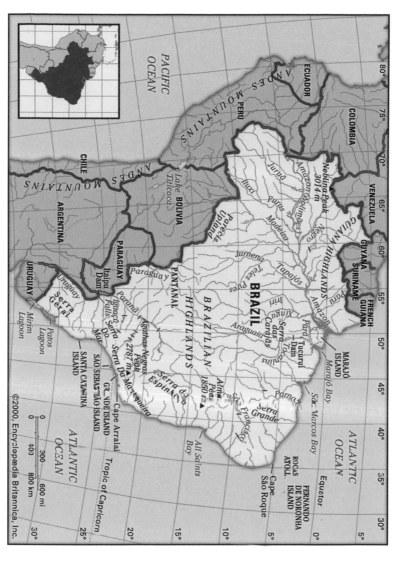

©2000, Encyclopædia Britannica, Inc.

Task Force Report

Overview

The United States now faces a Brazil that has undertaken a peaceful economic and social transformation to become the cornerstone of South American growth and stability and a significant power and presence on the world stage.[1]

The Task Force addresses its findings and recommendations not only to U.S. policymakers who focus on the Americas, but also to those in the United States and elsewhere who are responsible for decisions on the global strategic and economic issues and multilateral mechanisms in which Brazil's voice and actions are relevant. The findings and recommendations of this report provide a framework for bipartisan policies—global, regional, and bilateral—that take into account the opportunities and challenges of Brazil's rise as the United States and Brazil approach the major international issues of the twenty-first century.

WHY BRAZIL

Brazil is and will remain an integral force in the evolution of a multipolar world. It ranks as the world's fifth-largest landmass, fifth-largest population, and eighth-largest economy. Brazil, which may become the world's fifth-largest economy by 2016, is the B in the BRICs (along with Russia, India, and China*), a grouping of growth markets that accounted for 23 percent of global gross domestic product (GDP) in 2010 and will collectively reach $25 trillion to overtake the U.S. economy within the next decade. Brazil's economic prowess places it in a leadership position in Latin America and in the world and boosts the region's strategic importance globally, especially for the United States.

Given each country's landmass, economy, population, and resource base, Brazil and the United States necessarily interact in an increasingly

*South Africa formally joined the BRIC forum at the end of 2010, making it the BRICS forum.

globalized and multipolar world. Beyond the geostrategic characteristics that bring Brazil and the United States together, the two countries are also remarkably similar: both are multiethnic, young democracies that uphold common values with respect to free markets, rule of law, individual rights, religious freedom, and diversity and equality.

Despite these similarities, the U.S.-Brazil relationship has been prone to misunderstanding, and collaboration between the two countries has been limited. The election of Dilma Rousseff as Brazil's new president offers an opportunity for a renewed approach. Presidents Barack Obama and Rousseff have underscored a mutual desire to improve and deepen the relationship, and the Task Force urges that efforts be made by both countries to advance that goal. The Task Force believes that now is the time for the United States and Brazil to advance their foreign policy interests by reinvigorating and deepening this critical relationship.

OVERVIEW OF CORE CONCLUSIONS AND RECOMMENDATIONS

The Task Force recommends that U.S. policymakers recognize Brazil's standing as a global actor, treat its emergence as an opportunity for the United States, and work with Brazil to develop complementary policies.

Given Brazil's rise over the past two decades, the United States must now alter its view of the region and pursue a broader and more mature relationship with the new Brazil. It is time that the foreign policy of the United States reflects the new regional reality and adjusts to advance U.S. interests, given what has changed and the changes likely to come.

Brazil and the United States are now entering a period that has great potential to solidify a mature friendship, one that entails ever-deepening trust in order to secure mutual benefits. This kind of relationship requires the two countries to move beyond their historic oscillation between misinterpretation, public praise, and rebuke, and instead approach both cooperation and inevitable disagreement with mutual respect and tolerance.

The Task Force recommends open and regular communication between Obama and Rousseff and between senior officials of both countries. As Brazil continues to rise and the United States adapts to a multipolar order, frequent dialogue will help anticipate and diffuse tensions that will surface as each country reacts and adjusts to a new and evolving geopolitical dynamic. High-level contact will signal to each country's bureaucracy—historically distrustful of one another—that the relationship is a priority and that the success of each is in the other's interest.

Brazil's growing geostrategic importance merits sustained, senior-level, and comprehensive coordination of U.S. policy across agencies. The Task Force recommends that the National Security Council (NSC) institutionalize a standing interagency coordination mechanism so that a range of U.S. agencies responsible for functional issues—including finance, trade, labor, energy, environment, agriculture, health, homeland security, defense, and diplomacy—better coordinates what remains a highly decentralized U.S. policy toward Brazil.

This reorganization would require an NSC director for Brazil alone, rather than a director for Brazil and the Southern Cone. In addition, the Task Force recommends that the State Department create a separate Office for Brazilian Affairs outside the Office for Southern Cone Affairs. The goal is for a U.S. policy approach that treats Brazil as a global actor, with policies formulated not just by regional experts with narrow portfolios.

The Task Force encourages U.S. policymakers to recognize that independence will almost certainly remain a hallmark of Brazilian foreign policy, even as the two countries develop a closer relationship. Under Rousseff, Brazil likely will continue to engage—economically and diplomatically—in regions and on issues beyond the historic domain of South America. Brazilians will resist a tight U.S. embrace, and warming relations will not necessarily translate into Brazil's standing in line behind the United States. But the United States and Brazil can help each other advance mutual interests even without wholesale policy agreements between the two.

The Task Force finds that it is in the interest of the United States to welcome Brazil's regional leadership and encourage Brazil's promotion of inclusiveness, development, and democracy. Developing a more comprehensive U.S. policy toward Brazil should not come at the expense of deepening U.S. relationships with its other partners in the Americas.

The United States will need to adjust to a more assertive and independent Brazil. And Brazil must adjust to its new role as a global power. While the United States adapts to Brazil, it should also encourage Brazil to use its newfound multilateral and diplomatic influence in ways that look not only to its own national interests but to those of its neighbors and beyond.

Brazil and the United States face similar domestic challenges—including education, innovation, health care, and infrastructure—that should serve as an opportunity for deepening bilateral understanding and cooperation. The Task Force notes the critical importance of Brazil's continued progress in redressing its significant domestic constraints, which could jeopardize the sustainability of Brazil's long-term economic growth and deter its international ambitions.

The Task Force encourages both governments to maintain and expand channels of communication on trade and monetary policy, especially with respect to China. Brazil and the United States each approach China carefully, balancing relationships that are both complementary and competitive. Both Brazil and the United States have concerns about China's undervalued yuan, and though a joint approach is unrealistic, the Task Force suggests that Brazil and the United States agree on common language to describe the currency challenges presented by China in order to encourage China to allow its yuan to appreciate.

With an understanding of the divisive U.S. political environment, the Task Force encourages the U.S. Congress to include an elimination of the ethanol tariff in any bill regarding reform to the ethanol and biofuel tax credit regime.

The Task Force recommends that the Obama administration now fully endorse Brazil as a permanent member of the United Nations Security Council (UNSC). The Task Force encourages the administration to address important regional, multilateral, and global governance dimensions of such a step as it engages Brazil in an intense dialogue on this matter.

The Task Force report takes stock of Brazil's remarkable growth and development, including the domestic resources, constraints, and international factors that affect Brazil's economic trajectory. The report considers Brazil's approach to energy and climate change, both as relevant economic factors and as a means to help explain how Brazil conceives of its global role and how it aims to reshape world institutions. It examines Brazil's style, agenda, and growing engagement as a regional and global actor. Finally, the Task Force considers the U.S.-Brazil relationship and proposes ways in which the United States can work with and alongside Brazil to advance shared interests and common goals.

Introduction

Brazil has transcended its status as the largest and most resource-rich country in Latin America to now be counted among the world's pivotal powers. Brazil is not a conventional military power, it does not rival China or India in population or economic size, and it cannot match the geopolitical history of Russia. Still, how Brazil defines and projects its interests, a still-evolving process, is critical to understanding the character of the new multipolar and unpredictable global order.

Over the course of one generation, Brazil's domestic priority of inclusive growth has translated into a significant reduction of inequality, an expansion of the middle class, and a vibrant economy, all framed within a democratic context. These internal achievements drive Brazil's agenda on the world stage. Internationally, Brazil has leveraged its domestic assets and achievements to cement its role in areas as diverse as energy and climate change, peace and security, and trade and finance. Understanding and crafting a strategy to help in the success of this new Brazil is in the national interest of the United States.

CURRENT U.S. POLICY TOWARD BRAZIL

According to President Obama's recent statements, U.S. policy toward Brazil is based on engagement and "mutual interest and mutual respect," predicated on the belief that a strong relationship with Brazil promotes both U.S. and Brazilian interests. However, U.S. and Brazilian practice has not always matched this rhetoric. In a relationship that has more often been characterized by distance than by close friendship, substantive collaboration has been shallow and prone to misunderstanding.

Drawing upon groundwork laid by the Clinton and Bush administrations, the United States is now shaping a framework for a bilateral relationship with Brazil. Brazil and the United States do work together on a number of discrete issues, such as biofuels cooperation, defense, peacekeeping, and nonproliferation, among others.[2] Presidents Obama and Rousseff recently laid out an expanding agenda that includes civil aviation, space, innovation, science and technology, and education. Senior officials of the two countries occasionally maintain channels of communication on major international security issues. Still, for a variety of reasons, including competing priorities and domestic politics in each country, neither government has yet been able to weave the disparate threads of their joint ventures into the fabric of a cohesive strategic project.

The Task Force encourages Brazilian policymakers to draw upon the findings and recommendations of this report to inform their own decisions with respect to the United States. The new presidency in Brazil offers an opportunity to reset the relationship. The recent summit between presidents Obama and Rousseff in March 2011 underscored both countries' desire to improve and deepen this relationship.

The Task Force finds that it is in the interest of the United States to understand Brazil as a complex international actor whose influence on the defining global issues of the day is only likely to increase. Moreover, the success of Brazil's peaceful transformation—a project spanning two decades that has embraced democracy, markets, and robust social policy—is also in the United States' interest. Despite Brazil's rising prominence, the Task Force finds that the complexities and importance of Brazil are poorly understood and underestimated in Washington.

BRAZIL TODAY

The world watches with great interest as Rousseff attempts to build on the legacy of the enormously popular former president Luiz Inácio Lula da Silva (Lula) while charting her own course. Rousseff held two cabinet positions and served as Lula's chief of staff before being chosen as the ruling party's candidate. The daughter of a Bulgarian immigrant and a school teacher, Rousseff was jailed and tortured for her underground activism; she is an economist who had previously never run for election. Ambitious, results-driven, and pragmatic, Rousseff now stands as one of the most powerful and influential women in the world.

Former presidents Fernando Henrique Cardoso and Lula presided over sixteen years of democratic consolidation and sound economic policy. Brazil was well positioned to survive the global economic recession of 2008—having stabilized its currency, tackled rampant inflation, strengthened its banking system, and built up dollar reserves—and it emerged in 2009 relatively unscathed.

In a break from its past, Brazil's 2010 presidential election and recent political transition did not shake its strong stock market, bonds, or currency, signaling international confidence in its stability. Flows of foreign direct investment (FDI) into Brazil remain high: among non–Organization for Economic Cooperation and Development (OECD) countries, Brazil is second only to China as a destination for foreign investment. Though inflationary pressures remain a serious challenge, the Brazilian economy is expected to grow by more than 4 percent this year, after a particularly strong 2010 (7.5 percent growth).

The country Rousseff inherited in 2011 is substantially different from the one Lula inherited in 2003, as is the international environment. In the early stages of her presidency, Rousseff has stressed the need for Brazil's domestic agenda to drive and be served by the country's international engagement. In that vein, Brazil's foreign policy priorities under her leadership are likely to emphasize integrating with South America, establishing deeper ties and investment in Africa, managing a complex relationship with China, improving relations with the United States, and strengthening Brazil's influence in the restructuring of multilateral institutions.

The Brazilian economy is market based, though significant state involvement in shaping industrial policy remains a feature of Brazil's economic model. The Brazilian government's ownership and operation of major enterprises, its role as the primary source of capital and long-term local currency financing, its intervention in company decisions, and its high levels of social spending are all aspects of Brazil's development agenda. For example, the Rousseff administration has encouraged Brazil's largest private firms, known as national champions, to reinvest domestically, even at the expense of shareholder value. In addition, powerhouse companies (both Brazilian and foreign entities) in strategic sectors benefit from subsidized credit from the state-owned development bank (Banco Nacional de Desenvolvimento Econômico e Social—BNDES, or National Bank for Economic and Social Development). Brazilians across the ideological spectrum appear to accept and expect that the government will play a significant role as an investor, provider of social goods, and driver of growth.

Along with job creation from strong economic growth, large-scale social programs account for significant reductions in the levels of poverty, inequality, unemployment, and malnutrition—problems that dogged Brazil for decades and require continued attention. In particular, the federally instituted social welfare programs Fome Zero (Zero Hunger) and Bolsa Família (Family Allowance) and an increase in the minimum wage are largely credited for the significant social progress that Brazil has achieved over the past decade.[3] Between 2003 and 2009, Brazil's lower middle class, which now accounts for more than half of its total population, grew by almost thirty million people. This growing consumer class helps fuel a relatively diversified, albeit still commodities-dependent, economy.[4]

Brazil's immense and diverse territory is rich in natural resources. Exports of raw materials drive the Brazilian economy. Brazil is the world's largest producer of beef, cane sugar, and coffee and the second-largest producer of soybeans. Its agricultural strength is enhanced by its water resources and by technological achievements in adapting crops— soy, for example—to tropical conditions. In addition, Brazil is home to the world's sixth-largest proven uranium reserves, and its iron reserves rank among the world's top five.

Massive deposits of oil, discovered in 2006 off the coast of Rio de Janeiro, should place Brazil among the world's top ten energy producers in this decade. Brazil exported approximately fifty-seven thousand barrels per day of cane-based ethanol in 2009, rivaling—and, by some estimates, surpassing—the United States as an exporter.[5] Renewable resources supply almost 50 percent of Brazil's relatively clean energy matrix, with sugarcane-based products alone accounting for 19 percent of its total supply. Hydroelectricity also plays an important role in providing roughly 75 percent of Brazil's electricity. Water is both a source of renewable energy for Brazil and, given looming global water shortages, an important asset (especially as used to support agriculture). Brazil is home to 18 percent of the world's available fresh water, much of it derived from the Amazon River basin. The Amazon rainforest is itself a valuable resource, recycling carbon dioxide to produce more than 20 percent of the world's oxygen.

Despite Brazil's significant domestic achievements of social inclusion, steady growth, political stability, and use of its natural resources, major challenges loom. Indeed, some of the greatest could result from Brazil's assets and accomplishments. Brazil must manage to sustainably extract new oil reserves and navigate the political and social demands of distributing the benefits of its pending oil wealth, a process prone to politicization.

Although investments in education, innovation, and research and development are rising, Brazil does not yet have enough skilled laborers and professionals, even though Lula created more universities and technical schools than any president before him. A longstanding focus on higher education has strengthened Brazil's public universities, but the quality of public primary and secondary education remains poor. In addition to government efforts, Brazil's rich civil society—including an active media; an extensive web of labor, environmental, human rights, and religious organizations; and a private sector increasingly aware of the social and environmental implications of its ventures—acknowledges and works to meet these and other challenges.

Brazil remains the tenth most unequal country in the world, and more than one in four Brazilians still live below the poverty line. In Brazil's favelas, armed drug and criminal gangs preside over informal economies and extract a human and financial toll. The upcoming 2014 World Cup and the 2016 Olympic Games are expected to attract significant investment along with millions of visitors. But the events pose massive infrastructure, security, and public health challenges, and construction for the games is already lagging behind schedule. Underdeveloped infrastructure remains a significant problem in the vast territories of rural Brazil, which do not participate fully in the global economy and rarely feel the reach of the government. Despite intensified efforts to monitor the region, Brazil's porous nine-thousand-mile border remains vulnerable to illicit trade and transnational criminal networks.

Brazil's relationships with its ten bordering countries are just one complex aspect of the South American giant's wide-ranging and ambitious international agenda. Brazil's economic and domestic achievements, with respect to public health, hunger, poverty, inequality, clean energy, and environmental laws, constitute the basis for a robust Brazilian role within the UN, the World Health Organization (WHO), the Group of Twenty (G20), the World Bank, the International Monetary Fund (IMF), and international climate change negotiations. Over the past two decades, policy changes within a number of these organizations smoothed the way for Brazil's larger role within them. Brazil's

social programs have served as models for other such projects throughout the world.

This report does not attempt to explain, nor could it possibly do justice to, all of the aspects of Brazil's domestic and international profile.
The report instead focuses on four distinct but related issues that the
Task Force believes will, in large measure, determine Brazil's international and bilateral agenda in the near, medium, and long terms: the
Brazilian economy, including its engines and obstacles; Brazil's energy
and climate change profile; Brazil's track record, priorities, and ambitions as a global and regional diplomat; and Brazil's relationship with
the United States.

Brazil's Economy: Engines and Obstacles

Brazil's economic growth fuels its domestic achievements and much of its international agenda. Brazil's steadily growing economy propelled the South American giant into the global consciousness, initially among investors eyeing an emerging market. For Brazilians, the country's successful blend of capitalism and social democracy now justifies the promotion of these ideals and Brazil's economic interests abroad. Accordingly, Brazil has leveraged its domestic economic bona fides into international commercial and diplomatic power that it exercises across most regions of the world.

MACROECONOMICS IN TODAY'S BRAZIL

Sound macro policies, enhanced access to capital inflows, a transition from an import- to export-led economy, and a long period of favorable commodity prices and easy financing conditions have contributed to a profound economic and social transformation in recent years. Brazil's GDP per capita is now twice as high as it was ten years ago, and the poverty rate has been reduced by almost half.

President Rousseff entered office on the heels of a 7.5 percent economic growth in 2010, with expectations for a 4.5 percent expansion in 2011. The strong economic performance in 2010 was underpinned by robust domestic demand fueled by rapid credit growth and expansionary monetary and fiscal policy. The unemployment rate is at its lowest level in eight years, and real wages have increased sharply. Thus, although Brazil faces near-term challenges—mostly those associated with a rapidly growing economy—the long-term prospects for the country are positive, provided the abundance is managed appropriately.

However, the economic story is not without concerns. At the time of the writing of this report, inflationary pressures have grown noteworthy, and in major segments of the Brazilian economy some worry that overheating is taking place. Overheating pressures are manifesting themselves not only through higher inflation but also through a widening trade deficit and rapidly growing credit and asset prices.

There are also concerns that Brazil is now more vulnerable to major swings in global commodity prices; the country is too dependent on Asian demand for its future growth and thus would be vulnerable to setbacks in China and its neighbors; credit is growing rapidly, particularly in real estate markets such as the Rio and São Paulo regions, and asset prices may have worrisome bubble-like characteristics; and some important expected drivers of Brazilian expansion, such as tapping into pre-salt energy reserves, may take longer than anticipated to meet projections.

President Rousseff has made it clear that she is cognizant of these risks, and her appointments to head the Ministry of Finance and the Central Bank have a strong mandate to both offer critical continuity with the orthodox programs of the two preceding administrations and attend to these issues, of which the threat of inflation is increasingly seen as the most urgent. Indeed, a major source of consensus for macroeconomic policies lies in the shared Brazilian experience of rampant inflation in recent memory.

CHALLENGES AHEAD

The new government faces a wide range of economic challenges going forward that will require policy action. In the near term, the Brazilian government must remain attentive and resolute in its policies to avoid overheating and deal with the consequences of large capital inflows and a rapidly appreciating currency—the *real* has appreciated almost 40 percent against the dollar in the past two years—while trying to shape policies to protect and enhance the economic and social gains of the past decade.

Along with other major emerging-market countries, Brazil expressed concern about the U.S. Federal Reserve's decision to release $600 billion in an effort to stimulate the U.S. economy (the so-called QE2), a move that Brazilians feared would drive more money into countries with high interest rates as investors sought a higher return on their money. The negative Brazilian response was due partly to frustration with the absence of advance dialogue with the United States on monetary issues, and was also meant to balance simultaneous criticism of China. Among the tools used in response, Brazil raised its financial operations tax, known as the IOF, on foreign purchases of local bonds.

Brazil stands out in its region for a relatively high level of public debt, high public revenues, and low public investment. Between 2005 and 2008, for example, Brazil's public sector invested, in terms of GDP, half of what Argentina, Chile, Colombia, Mexico, Peru, and Uruguay did. Improvements in this area will not be easy and will require fundamental changes in fiscal strategies. The country's poor quality of physical infrastructure, for example, reflects this low level of public investment. To prepare for the World Cup in 2014 and the Olympics in 2016, Brazil has, however, begun to undertake a high-priority program to improve infrastructure. Labor, pension, and social security reform—issues that need to be tackled by the Rousseff administration—would greatly improve public savings and provide more flexibility for other spending priorities.

Doing business and forming small and medium-sized businesses in Brazil remains a challenge given the complexity of the tax system, high labor and corporate taxes, and the slow processes of judicial review for contract enforcement—issues that the Brazilian government itself acknowledges as obstacles. Brazil's complex regulatory, tax, and protectionist regimes hamper foreign investment and slow the conditions for even more robust and equitable growth. As in the United States, addressing such structural challenges in Brazil is difficult because of domestic politics at the federal, state, and municipal levels. Trade policy will also test the Rousseff administration. Brazil is in the early stages of developing, among its small and medium-sized businesses, the facility for and the inclination to view foreign trade as a driver of growth and development.

Conclusions
The Task Force notes that, in this context, near-term attention to the threats of inflation and overheating more broadly is warranted. In 2010, inflation reached 5.8 percent, well above the 4.5 percent target. Nonetheless, the Task Force finds that the Rousseff administration—which has pursued a round of budget cuts, raised interest rates, and taken steps to regulate consumer credit—has reacted prudently, although even greater attention to these concerns and a greater willingness to

acknowledge threats earlier is warranted. This is also an area, given the importance of Brazil's economy globally, in which it is in the interests of the United States and other G20 powers to work closely with Brazil to avoid problems that may produce significant contagion regionally and worldwide.

BRAZIL'S TRADE AND INVESTMENT RELATIONSHIP WITH CHINA: RISKS AND REWARDS

Brazil's economic relations with China are at once mutually beneficial, competitive, and a real challenge to the long-term diversification of the Brazilian economy. Trade and investment were the focus of Rousseff's visit to China in April 2011, the first major foreign trip of her presidency. Brazil has gained considerably from its trade and investment relations with China over the past decade. Commodity prices reached record-high levels driven mainly by the impressive growth of the Chinese economy and its demand for natural resources. In the first two quarters of 2010, China became the primary buyer of Brazilian exports, ahead of the United States, and the number-two source of Brazilian imports, behind the United States.

This increase in trade flows, however, has triggered an imbalanced relationship, generating increasing concern among Brazilian policymakers and the private sector about deindustrialization. As of the first quarter of 2010, approximately 79 percent of Brazilian exports to China consisted of basic goods and raw materials (soy, iron ore, and oil), but more than 90 percent of imports from China were capital or manufactured goods. In 2009, the industrial sector share of Brazil's GDP fell to 15.5 percent, the lowest figure since 1947. Many in Brazil are concerned that loose monetary conditions in the United States and large foreign exchange interventions in China have caused the real to soar against the dollar and the yuan, and cheap Chinese imports have damaged the country's manufacturing base.

As part of China's broader strategy to secure natural resources in the developing world, China became Brazil's leading investor in 2010, with estimates of $12 billion to $20 billion invested primarily in the steel, oil, mining, transportation, and energy sectors. The upcoming World Cup and the Olympic Games, as well as the need to explore newfound reserves of oil offshore, are drawing more Chinese investments to Brazil, particularly for infrastructure projects. In Brazil, concern is increasing over whether China will abide by market rules, in particular with respect to real estate and intellectual property rights.

Brazil's investments in China are much more modest, but relevant nonetheless as Brazilian companies move to China to target Chinese consumers and to use the country as an export platform to other regions, including to Brazil itself. Still, some Brazilian national champions—themselves supported by low-cost, government financing—cannot compete with even more heavily subsidized Chinese companies. For example, the Brazilian aircraft manufacturer Embraer, which has a factory in China, competes with a Chinese regional maker whose plane resembles the Brazilian model.

The Rousseff administration has identified its relationship with China as one of its major strategic challenges. As Brazil-China asymmetries persist, trade deals with other major economies—notably the European Union (talks are already under way) and the United States—will become more attractive to Brazil. In her first several months in office, Rousseff has moderated Lula's criticism of U.S. monetary policy, and the Task Force expects Rousseff to seek closer ties to the United States to balance China. U.S. treasury secretary Timothy F. Geithner, who visited São Paulo and Brasília in advance of the February 2011 G20 meeting of finance ministers, emphasized the impact of Chinese monetary policy on both economies during his discussions in Brazil.

Conclusions and Recommendations

China and Brazil are helping fuel each other's growth, meet each other's needs, and thus strengthen each other's international position. The Brazil-China partnership is likely to be one that grows significantly stronger in the years ahead and, as is often the case, the Task Force expects deepening and extensive economic ties to create an incentive for greater political and diplomatic coordination. The Task Force recognizes that the growing importance of this relationship with China enhances Brazil's ability and inclination to act independently of the views of the United States and other neighbors in this hemisphere.

Both Brazil and the United States have an interest in mitigating volatility in emerging economies. The Task Force acknowledges Brazil's forcefully stated concern that the United States' second quantitative easing and China's artificial undervaluing of the yuan attracts hot money to Brazil, drives up the value of Brazil's real, and adds overheating pressures in the form of higher inflation, a widening trade deficit, and rapidly growing credit and asset prices. With the slowness of the U.S. recovery, U.S. interests are, for the moment at least, divergent to some degree, and Brazil and the United States are not likely to be able to consistently coordinate monetary policy closely, because both countries are sensitive first and foremost to their domestic circumstances and constituencies. Nonetheless, the Task Force finds that Brazil's escalating criticism of Chinese monetary policy illustrates an alignment between Brazilian and U.S. concerns and thus provides an opportunity for greater cooperation and coordination between Brazil and the United States going forward.

The Task Force encourages both governments to maintain and expand channels of communication on monetary policy, especially with respect to China, in an effort to reinforce the message that a floating Chinese currency would be beneficial to the global economy. Brazil and the United States each approach China carefully, balancing relationships that are both complementary and competitive. The Task Force suggests that Brazil and the United States agree to common language to describe challenges of China's undervalued currency, in order to underscore their shared concern.

DOMESTIC ASSETS

For generations, abundant and varied economic resources have promised to bring prosperity to Brazil. In the 1970s, Brazil looked poised to break into the ranks of the world's wealthiest nations. But by 1982, the so-called Brazilian economic miracle had withered with the onset of the Latin American debt crisis. Now, however, Brazil's expertise in tropical agriculture and its growing mineral resource production have coincided with rising global commodities prices and demand.

Brazil is again well positioned to make productive use of its natural endowments. Income from and jobs generated by natural resources will likely continue to expand the middle class and sustain domestic growth, helping boost Brazil's economy from the world's eighth-largest to the fifth-largest as early as 2016. Over the next decade, Brazil's domestic development will rest on four pillars of growth: agriculture, mining and metallurgy, a growing middle class, and energy production.[6]

AGRICULTURE

Brazil uses its agricultural might and knowhow to ensure food security both at home and overseas. Brazil is the fourth-largest exporter of food globally; a world leader in staples like soy, sugarcane, coffee, and beef; and a major producer of a wide range of items including tobacco, cotton, orange juice, and cashews. As a country just shy of 200 million people, Brazil produces enough food to meet the minimum caloric requirements of about 250 million. Though 10 million Brazilian citizens still lack food security, this figure is a 75 percent reduction from a decade earlier and is due in large part to the success of the Fome Zero program and strong economic growth. Much of the credit also goes to Brazilian advances in agricultural technology.

Brazilian agricultural innovations have made agriculture more efficient and have expanded farming to parts of the country where crops could not grow roughly a decade ago, converting Brazil into an agriculture powerhouse with industrial-scale farming. The Brazilian Agricultural Research Corporation (Empresa Brasileira de Pesquisa Agropecuária, known as Embrapa) has worked since its inception in 1973 to develop new farmland and has modified varieties of seeds to grow in those environments.[7] Agriculture now makes up a quarter of Brazilian GDP and accounts for 40 percent of export revenue. According to some estimates, pastureland covers nearly 25 percent of the country and 150 million acres of arable land remain uncultivated.

Within the framework of the BRICS countries, Brazil has become integral to the international effort to mitigate problems of food production and hunger, which has included a commitment to develop a joint strategy to ensure access to food for vulnerable populations. Cooperation is strongest in Africa. Embrapa África, in conjunction with the Brazilian Agency for Cooperation (ABC), has personnel stationed in Ghana, Mozambique, Senegal, and Mali to coordinate food security programs, which generates goodwill for Brazil and an opportunity for cooperation with the United States. Initiatives under way from Latin America to the Middle East to Oceania point to Brazil's global ambitions.

Conclusions and Recommendations

The Task Force finds that Brazil's technological innovation in agriculture has allowed the country to capitalize on its natural resources and global economic conditions in order to carve out a place for itself on the world stage. Moreover, with more than one billion people under-nourished worldwide, Brazil's growing contribution to global food stores makes it a fundamental part of any international approach to food security.

Brazil and the United States are among the largest agricultural producers and exporters in the world. Agricultural technologies developed by U.S. companies are already being used to improve land productivity in Brazil, and barriers to further expansion (to the extent that any remain) are the subject of bilateral government discussions. The Task Force encourages the U.S. Department of Agriculture (USDA) to enhance capacity for cooperation on innovation and deployment of new technologies and development of standards. The USDA should provide funds for U.S. scientists to work with their counterparts in the Brazilian Embrapa. In addition, the Task Force recommends that the USDA consult with Embrapa in the development of genetically modified organisms (GMOs) to ensure that U.S. products meet Brazilian standards.

MINING AND METALLURGY

Mineral extraction provides Brazil with the material to address the country's infrastructure deficit and also serves as a major source of national revenue. The country produces and exports significant amounts of nickel, copper, bauxite, iron ore, and other elements of common alloys like steel. Indeed, Brazil is the world's third-largest producer of bauxite (used in the most cost-effective method of producing aluminum) and the ninth-largest producer of steel. It is increasing its steel production with investment from Chinese and U.S. companies and boosting exports through new plants and ports. Like its agriculture, Brazil's mineral assets are a valuable commodity that makes Brazil a vital trading partner for any member of the international community, especially those poised for infrastructure-dependent growth.

GROWING MIDDLE CLASS AND DOMESTIC DEMAND

Perhaps the largest component of Brazil's economic growth at home is its expanding middle class. Bolsa Familia, Fome Zero, subsidized loans for housing, and an increase in the minimum wage (which rose 62 percent in real terms under Lula) have lifted an estimated thirty million people out of poverty in the past eight years. Though more than ten million Brazilians (5.21 percent of the population) live on less than $1.25 per day and Brazil remains the third most unequal country in Latin America, Brazil's Gini coefficient has declined from 0.61 to 0.54 since 2001.

The greatest and fastest-paced increase in incomes is occurring among Brazilians in the *clase C*, Brazil's middle or consumer class.[8] In 2009, 61.1 percent of all Brazilians were members of classes A, B, or C, up from 37.9 percent in 2003. The aggregate purchasing power of *clase C* is responsible for between 31 and 46 percent of the Brazilian economy. *Clase C* consumers make up the largest discrete economic group in Brazil.[9] In stark contrast to China, Brazil has seen lower incomes grow at substantially faster rates than higher incomes over the past decade, accounting for shrinking income inequality.

As the middle classes have grown in size and prosperity, their spending habits have shifted as well. According to the 2010 Brazilian census, 69 percent of Brazil's middle class own their own homes; more than 20 percent own a car; 89 percent have mobile phones; 50 percent own computers (more than 30 percent of whom have broadband connections); and all have televisions. Brazil's manufacturing base largely sells to this internal market (indeed, the Ministry of Development, Industry, and Foreign Trade encourages Brazilian businesses to export more), but some Brazilian goods are being priced out by Chinese imports.

Expansion of credit has underpinned rising Brazilian purchasing power. Though the share of domestic credit in the Brazilian economy appears low (at about 46 percent of GDP, compared with 80 percent in Chile) given its level of income, Brazilian borrowers pay a relatively high interest rate of 20 to 25 percent. As new consumers rapidly take on debt, monetary policy authorities in Rousseff's administration are keenly aware of the risk of excess leverage and are taking steps to tighten credit.

Conclusions
Brazil has deliberately created an environment in which upward mobility is within the reach of the vast majority of its population. Brazil's domestic market is a crucial driver of the country's economy and will attract an increasing number of international partners, in the region and abroad, who hope to gain greater access to Brazilian consumers. In light of the contributions of the housing debt crisis to the U.S. financial crisis, the Task Force finds that ensuring the financial literacy of and

developing savings vehicles for Brazil's newest consumers will be critical to preventing their financial overstretch and possible damage to Brazil's growth prospects.

DOMESTIC CONSTRAINTS

Brazil's successes in meeting long-standing challenges such as poverty and inequality are undeniable. At the same time, Brazil's swelling middle class, substantial deepwater oil finds, and upcoming major international sporting events raise expectations and create new challenges for Brazil. Its major undertakings for the next decade are to absorb and build on its achievements and reduce remaining social deficits. How Brazil fares on these counts will significantly influence its economic growth and ultimately will affect how it projects itself internationally.

Brazil's ability to compete over the long term on the world stage, with the likes of China and India, depends on improving infrastructure, elevating the quality of basic education, increasing the number of skilled laborers who supply burgeoning Brazilian industries, and creating socially and environmentally sustainable conditions in which innovation and small businesses can flourish. If it cannot meet these challenges, it risks falling behind.

The stakes for Brazil are high: popular expectations of a progressive and positive trajectory place great pressure on Brazil's democratically elected leaders. In light of its experience of hyperinflation, inequality, poverty, and social exclusion, backsliding could have profound and negative implications for the health of its democracy and social contract.

INFRASTRUCTURE

Brazil requires massive investment across the spectrum of basic infrastructure to meet current needs and to maintain its recent rapid pace of growth. Forty-three percent of Brazilian households—some 25 million families—live in inadequate housing without consistent access to clean water, sewage disposal, and garbage collection. Brazil's aging seaports handle 95 percent of Brazil's exports, yet are ranked 123 out of 139 countries in the World Economic Forum's most recent global competitiveness report. The lack of an integrated national rail system forces most producers in the interior to send their goods to port via trucks, but only 10 percent of the nation's roads—accounting for roughly 124,000 miles crossing a country of more than 3 million square miles—are paved.

Airports are also overwhelmed, with seven of the country's top twenty airports experiencing frequent congestion delays; São Paulo's international airport is ranked third worst in the world for flight delays. Telecommunications saw significant investment following privatization a decade ago, allowing mobile phone use to increase to nearly eight hundred accounts per thousand people by 2008, leapfrogging fixed land lines that had just three hundred accounts per thousand.

Rousseff was the architect of the R$642 billion Program to Accelerate Growth (PAC, implemented from 2007 to 2010), and its nearly R$1 trillion successor PAC II (covering 2011 through 2014), which seek to address these infrastructure shortcomings. Increased electricity generation capacity accounts for nearly half of the proposed PAC II budget, housing and transportation a further 40 percent and water, sewage, and urban infrastructure the remaining 10 percent. If fully implemented, PAC II would go far toward boosting Brazil's investment in infrastructure above its historical 2 percent of GDP toward the 4 to 5 percent many analysts suggest is required to maintain rapid economic growth. Brazil's northeast, which receives significant infrastructure investment from the government (for example, the Suape port complex outside of Recife), is the country's fastest-growing region, expanding at a rate of 2 percentage points higher than the rest of the country.

Full implementation is not ensured, however. The original PAC suffered from implementation delays, and only 40 percent of the earmarked funds were spent by the end of 2009, although election-year stimulus boosted PAC spending to 74 percent of the proposed total. Major projects related to the 2014 World Cup and 2016 Olympics, such as a high-speed rail line between São Paulo and Rio de Janeiro, are significantly delayed. Project costs and capacity constraints, in the physical labor available to complete projects and in BNDES's ability to complete project financing, will likely increase as critical dates approach.

The politicization of major projects and the lack of suitable financing outside BNDES (commercial banks are unable to provide funding at the interest rate, tenor, and volume required) limit the number of concurrent initiatives that can be undertaken and slow the development of projects once they are approved. Indeed, BNDES's own February 2011 assessment of near-term infrastructure investment identified only

R$380 billion worth of projects in electricity generation, telecommunications, sanitation, and transportation between 2011 and 2014.

Conclusions and Recommendations

As the upcoming host of both the 2014 World Cup and the 2016 Olympics, Brazil has a unique opportunity to leverage these events to push urban infrastructure to the top of its national agenda in a manner that supports strong economic growth and promotes sustainable development. Rio de Janeiro in particular offers an opportunity to anticipate critical long-term urban infrastructure needs in a rapidly developing megacity and leverage compressed investment timelines to establish a template for building the green economies and smart cities of the future, including in the United States. However, it will be important that these investments be carried out without adding to overheating pressures.

U.S. and Brazilian industry, working in partnership with federal and local government agencies, would be well positioned to deliver innovative solutions to the challenges of city-scale infrastructure investment. The Task Force welcomes the development of the U.S.-Brazil Joint Initiative on Urban Sustainability (JIUS), as envisioned by the Environmental Protection Agency (EPA) and formally initiated during Obama's trip to Brazil in March 2011.

The Task Force encourages interagency support for and progress on JIUS, which works to identify and support sector-specific infrastructure investment opportunities in transportation, air quality, water and wastewater, energy, waste, and land redevelopment infrastructure projects. JIUS will leverage planned event investments and focus on green growth and sustainability as a means of jointly ensuring a green, smart, and energy-efficient build-up of major Brazilian infrastructure in advance of major world events.

EDUCATION

Access to public education for primary and secondary students eluded Brazil for much of its history. The social welfare program Bolsa Familia has fostered record primary and secondary school enrollment. But by age twelve, Brazilian students, girls especially, begin dropping out; the rate rapidly accelerates at age sixteen, the legal age for formal employment. The quality of public education remains poor and highly variable by state, location within a city, and socioeconomic status. According to

Brazilian national education assessments, between 1995 and 2007, no significant improvement was observed in the levels of learning by Brazilian students in the grades analyzed.

During the same period, Brazil dedicated significant resources to education: conditional cash transfers were first linked with school attendance in 2001, and education spending increased by 66 percent between 2000 and 2007, according to the OECD. Brazil's public expenditure on education as a percentage of GDP (5.2 percent) is comparable to U.S. spending (5.5 percent) and greater than Russia, India, and China. Yet Brazil ranks well below these other emerging economies in math, science, and reading indicators. Indeed, of the 139 countries reviewed by the World Economic Forum for competitiveness, the overall quality of Brazil's primary education system was ranked 127. Brazil fared similarly poorly in a December 2010 OECD cross-country study, though it did show marginal improvement in quality of math and science education.[10]

Historically, Brazil has spent more heavily on higher education. Still, the number of vocational and technical schools in Brazil falls well short of satisfying Brazilian demand for skilled labor.[11] Public vocational and technical schools, which expanded under Lula, make up approximately 30 percent of all such institutions. Brazilian tertiary institutions are not training enough students to produce high value-added goods. Private companies often have to educate their own employees. As of 2007, nearly 80 percent (four of every five) of skilled laborers in Brazil undertook a firm-based training program. In a country with massive infrastructure needs, in 2008 only 6 percent of master's and doctoral degrees were in engineering and architecture. Likewise, only 13 percent of university graduates studied in a science-related field in 2010.

Brazilians often acknowledge that perhaps the most important challenge now before them is to provide universal and quality public education in its primary, secondary, and vocational schools. The Brazilian government has set a target of reaching OECD-education levels by 2021. Brazil's education ministry and a public-private coalition supporting the UNESCO project Educação para Todos (Education for All) have committed to a spending target of 7 percent of GDP by 2015. Alongside these efforts, Todos pela Educação (Everyone for Education), a movement financed by the private sector, works to bring together civil society organizations, educators and school systems, and public officials to ensure quality basic education for all Brazilian youth by 2022.

Conclusions and Recommendations
The Task Force finds that Brazil's long-term ability to uphold its social contract, sustain its economic trajectory, and solidify its standing as a global power depends on the development of an improved and integrated education system at the primary and secondary levels. An improved education system would not only retain students but also provide quality education with access to opportunities in the workplace and in tertiary education. Likewise, Brazil's continued economic growth depends on the country's ability to convert its massive consumer class into a producing one that supports labor demands and generates innovation. This, in turn, requires more efficient investment in all levels of public education and a focus on science and engineering in tertiary education institutions.

As concern about education quality and reform increases in both the United States and Brazil, the Task Force encourages the U.S. Department of Education and leading U.S. practitioners to engage with their Brazilian counterparts and the Brazilian Ministry of Education to share lessons learned and best practices, including the U.S. community college model. The Task Force recommends increased research and exchange partnerships between U.S. and Brazilian universities and academic institutions across a range of subject areas, particularly in fields related to engineering, math and sciences, and international relations.

The Task Force encourages the U.S. Department of State's Bureau of Educational and Cultural Affairs to increase the funding available (through initiatives like the Fulbright program) for American scholars to work and teach in Brazil and for Brazilian counterparts to study and teach in the United States, which requires increased flexibility and timeliness in granting of visas. The Task Force also recommends additional State and Defense Department funding for Portuguese-language programs.

INNOVATION

Fostering innovation and enterprise is squarely on the domestic and international agenda of the Brazilian government. Indeed, the Ministry of Science and Technology has acknowledged and begun to address Brazil's deficit in innovation. The Brazilian government also recognizes the importance of technology transfer from abroad as an engine of domestic innovation and growth. Trends are positive as, over the past five years, the Brazilian government has moved toward the commercial-ization of innovation, shifting away from the state-based investment in science and technology that characterized the military era and has since remained. For example, the Rousseff administration has moved to privatize Brazil's civil aviation industry, which has traditionally been controlled by the military.

Research and development (R&D) are underfunded in Brazil rela-tive to other countries, and the funding that is in place does not pro-duce results at the rates seen elsewhere.[12] Notably, Brazil and South Korea had similar levels of GDP per capita thirty years ago. Today, however, South Korea has grown to be more than three times richer than Brazil (in purchasing power parity terms). South Korea invests more than 3 percent of its GDP in innovation; in Brazil the figure is just over 1 percent.

Brazil's historic and current comparative advantage in commodi-ties has itself distorted the incentive structure for innovation. In 2000, manufactured goods accounted for nearly 60 percent of Brazil's exports, and primary goods totaled just over 20 percent. In 2009, pri-mary goods overtook manufactured goods—a reversal that starkly illustrates the growing competitive disadvantage. The sheer volume of foreign demand, from India and especially China, for raw goods like soya, iron ore, and beef drives Brazil's growing emphasis on commodi-ties exporting.

The quality of science education and know-how in Brazilian aca-demia is strong, but the gulf between the academy and ideas reaching the market is large. At universities, leading academics tend to view a disconnection between the scholarly research they conduct and the commercial application of their results. Academia is not viewed as an instrument of economic development as it is in Boston or San Fran-cisco, for example.

Brazil's inefficient and complex regulatory environment—along with poor infrastructure, inadequate education, high and complex taxes, and rigid labor requirements—make it costly and difficult to com-mercialize new technology and start new businesses in Brazil. Accord-ing to the World Bank, it takes 120 days to register a business in Brazil, compared with twenty-two in Chile and just six in the United States.

A tradition of heavy state involvement in industry from the time of Brazil's independence, through industrialization, and up to the present day has led Brazilians to look to the state for guidance in what and how to produce. Brazil's Financing Agency for Studies and Projects (FINEP, associated with the Ministry of Science and Technology) has an annual budget of approximately $2.5 billion to fund scientific and technological development, from R&D for large companies to local innovation systems. Annually, FINEP provides financing for three thousand companies in Brazil (both domestic and foreign), the majority of which are start-ups. Moreover, some parastatal companies have themselves been sources of innovation and demonstrate Brazil's ability to become a world-class innovator in certain scientific and technical sectors.

Brazil increased its agricultural productivity via Embrapa and built the world's second-largest biofuels industry, as a result of Pro-alcool, the government's ethanol promotion program. State-controlled Petrobras has likewise emerged at the forefront of deep-sea oil drilling technology. The Fundação Oswaldo Cruz (Fiocruz), a state-funded public health institution, and its Farmanguinhos and Bio-Manguinhos programs in particular, are world-class examples of innovation in the health sector. These successes suggest that state-driven industrial policy can yield significant results on a large scale, although economists are divided over the long-term benefits of state-directed industrial policies. Although Brazil lacks a strong culture of private innovation, individual entrepreneurship is common—one of every eight adults has created his or her own business, one of the highest rates in the world, though many of these businesses are likely outside the formal economy.

Conclusions and Recommendations

The Task Force finds that low levels of innovation in Brazil and a dearth of mechanisms needed to foster innovation hamper the country's potential over the long run.[13] The legacy of heavy state intervention in industry will be hard to overcome, and, indeed, many Brazilians prefer the status quo. Though a drastic shift in the culture of innovation is unlikely in the near term, the Brazilian government can pursue steps to encourage small and medium-sized businesses by beginning to simplify government bureaucracy and by promoting private-sector collaboration with the nation's universities.

The Task Force urges action within the U.S. Congress to allow technology transfer to accompany Brazilian purchases of U.S. military equipment. These transfers would boost bilateral trade, U.S. industry, and defense cooperation and simultaneously support Brazil's technology and innovation agenda.

Brazil's investment in health research is providing tangible benefits and important successes in developing interventions for disease, including HIV/AIDS and the so-called neglected diseases that disproportionally affect low- and middle-income countries (such as malaria, tuberculosis, and leprosy). The Task Force encourages the U.S. Department of Health and Human Services and the National Institutes of Health to foster partnerships with their Brazilian counterparts to help build global health capacity and collaborate in scientific research projects that could help generate novel diagnostics, therapeutics, and vaccines.

Brazil's Energy and Climate Change Agenda

Brazil's energy and environmental profiles have established it as a major international actor on two of the most central and intimately linked global challenges: energy security and climate change. With as many as 50 billion barrels of oil beneath Brazilian waters, 167 million barrels of annual ethanol production (and plans to increase output to more than 400 million barrels by 2019), hydroelectric dams that supply as much as 75 percent of Brazilian electricity, and the world's sixth-largest proven uranium reserves, Brazil is poised to become a significant exporter of diverse energy products.

A looming oil boom has generated significant international interest. The Brazilian energy company Petrobras raised $70 billion in 2010 in the world's largest public share offering. Brazil's pre-salt finds (oil held in rocks beneath a salt layer deep off Brazil's coast) are destined to markedly influence Brazil's economy and politics, and perhaps its environment as well.

The Brazilian energy matrix is among the least carbon intensive of the major economies, and Brazil has made voluntary commitments to reduce carbon output and deforestation (although the rate of deforestation remains significant). The path to a lower-carbon economy requires significant investment (in incentives to prevent deforestation, for example) that could increase GDP and employment, though Brazilians remain concerned that sustainability efforts will hamper growth.[14]

Monitoring and enforcement of climate and deforestation legislation remain difficult and imperfect. Still, energy and environmental issues provide Brazil with its most substantial platform for international influence.

ENERGY

Brazil's energy matrix is among the least carbon intensive of the major economies because the majority of its electricity is provided by hydropower and other renewable fuels; sugar-based ethanol also provides a large share of transportation fuels.[15] Brazil is also developing its substantial hydrocarbon and uranium resources.

Brazil's energy position and low level of carbon intensity will be challenging to maintain. Continued industrialization and rising standards of living have created an energy demand that outpaces Brazil's existing infrastructure. The resulting pressure on the country's energy infrastructure requires continuous development within all segments of the energy value chain. Perhaps the biggest challenge is for Brazil to do so while maintaining renewable energy's share of the energy mix, currently at 50 percent.

Labor and land-use concerns, including the potential impact on biodiversity in the Cerrado and Amazon, challenge continued growth in ethanol production.[16] At the same time, electricity production is diversifying away from hydropower toward greater natural-gas-fired generation, as most new large-capacity sites are located far from demand centers or in environmentally sensitive areas such as the Amazon.

Conclusions and Recommendations
The Task Force finds that energy is and will remain a critical component of Brazil's economic and political agenda, driven by rising per capita energy consumption, development of substantial domestic energy resources, and the need to expand existing energy infrastructure. Brazil's investment in this industry is a primary example of its domestic and international agendas reinforcing each other. The United States and Brazil have common interests in improving energy efficiency, reducing carbon intensity, promoting the development of biofuels, expanding the use of natural gas, and managing offshore oil exploration and development.

The Task Force applauds the formation of a bilateral Strategic Energy Dialogue, announced by Obama and Rousseff, to address a broad range of energy issues, including the safe and sustainable development of Brazil's deepwater oil and gas resources, as well as cooperation on biofuels and other renewals, energy efficiency, and civilian nuclear energy. The dialogue aims to encourage energy partnerships, create jobs in both countries, make energy supplies more secure, and help address the challenge of climate change.[17] The Task Force urges both countries to ensure that this initiative becomes a self-sustaining endeavor that brings together government officials, regulators, and the private sector to engage in conversation, cooperation, and collaboration where appropriate.

PRE-SALT DEPOSITS

The opening of the oil sector to competition in 1997 and partial privatization of Petrobras ushered in an era of rapid growth in oil production and exploration investment. Privatization of many of the state-owned power distribution and generation companies during the same period also boosted investment in distribution networks and new power-generation capacity. Brazil's oil production more than doubled after liberalization, reaching 2.6 million barrels per day in 2009 and transforming Brazil from an oil importer to a net exporter. Petrobras remains the dominant actor in the industry but is joined by more than forty domestic and international companies actively investing in the nearly five hundred upstream exploration and production blocks that have been auctioned to date.

The 2006 discovery of the Tupi field in the pre-salt formation opened one of the world's most important new oil frontiers. According to Brazil's national oil regulator, Agência Nacional do Petróleo, pre-salt reserves could hold as many as fifty billion to eighty billion barrels of recoverable hydrocarbons—potentially six times Brazil's current proven reserves of just under thirteen billion barrels.[18] If proven, these estimates would place Brazil among the world's ten largest oil reserve holders, or in the range between those of Russia and Venezuela. The pre-salt reserves have the potential to make Brazil a major global oil exporter.[19] Pre-salt oil may begin flowing in large volumes over the next five to seven years. According to optimistic predictions, Brazil may produce up to four million barrels of oil per day by 2010, one million barrels as net exports.[20]

Brazil is one of just a few countries in the Western Hemisphere—Canada being another—that will significantly increase oil production over the next decade. Despite the difficulties of doing business in Brazil, the Brazilian oil sector is one of only a handful of attractive resource bases in the world that welcomes foreign investment. Indeed, in late

2010, Petrobras raised $70 billion in the world's largest share offering. However, the capitalization raised some concerns of politicization as the government assumed even greater control of Petrobras and minority shareholder value diminished.

The pre-salt deposits hold great promise, but many daunting challenges remain. The reservoir's geophysical characteristics and its position below miles of salt and water make it technically difficult to develop. Its location more than three hundred kilometers offshore—a distance too great to supply via helicopter without an interim staging platform—and its relatively high share of carbon dioxide and associated natural gas greatly increase the logistical complexity of producing the oil. Brazil's revised oil law designates Petrobras as the operator in any development and imposes strict local content requirements. This will put an unprecedented strain on the ability of both Petrobras and the country in general to supply the required capital, raw materials, equipment, and management and manpower capabilities.

Concern about the risks of too many simultaneous projects and deteriorating investment climates has led Petrobras to scale back its activities in South America, focusing on domestic investments and new projects in West Africa, the U.S. Gulf, and Australia, where Petrobras's deepwater capabilities provide synergies and a competitive advantage.

Finally, Brazil's politicians continue to debate how best to divide and spend the government revenues that are anticipated to come from pre-salt development. Notably, 50 percent of pre-salt oil revenues will support state-run socioeconomic programs. In the past, the states that held the physical resource received the lion's share of oil revenues. The new pre-salt regime proposes more even sharing among all Brazilian states, benefiting the interior and poorer states in the northeast at the expense of Rio de Janeiro and São Paulo. The final details remain to be worked out within the enabling legislation and regulations that will build on the basic legal framework enacted in 2010.

Conclusions and Recommendations

As Brazil develops its pre-salt oil and thereby diversifies global energy suppliers, the Task Force considers greater oil exports from Brazil to be in the United States' strategic interest. As the United States seeks to diversify its energy supply, increased imports from Brazil could help reduce its dependency on exports from less stable countries. Though the United States will not have a significant influence on the trajectory of pre-salt development, the Ex-Im Bank, the Overseas Private Investment Corporation, and the U.S. Trade and Development Agency can provide financing to U.S. companies to facilitate their participation.

The Task Force recognizes that Brazil's pre-salt oil will have a dramatic effect on Brazil as the country reinvents itself as an energy power and develops a regulatory and distribution framework that corresponds to Brazilian priorities.

Given the 2010 deepwater oil accident and spill in the U.S. Gulf of Mexico, the Task Force is mindful of the risks of deep-sea drilling. Developing this resource poses significant technical, logistical, environmental, and political challenges, and the timing and pace of production growth is uncertain. The Task Force encourages the U.S. government to convey the lessons learned from the BP Macondo well disaster and welcomes the government-sponsored workshop series that was formed in early 2011 by the United States and Brazil to share best practices on safe development of offshore resources. The United States can build on this existing bilateral mechanism to launch a multilateral effort that includes relevant private sector and government participants from other deepwater producers such as Norway, Australia, Nigeria, Angola, and other emerging producers in Africa.

NATURAL GAS

Natural gas consumption, which accounts for just 9 percent of Brazil's energy use, compared with 24 percent in the United States, is increasing rapidly, driven by expanding gas-fired power generation and growing industrial demand. Two floating liquefied natural gas terminals allow Brazil to import gas from beyond its neighbors (supplies from South America, though sufficient, tend to be less reliable). The Task Force notes that Petrobras's dominance in the gas sector has prevented the development of a competitive domestic gas market and may hamper efforts to diversify sources of electricity generation.

Brazil imports roughly 25 percent of the gas it consumes from Bolivia—a relationship once strained by Bolivia's 2006 nationalization of its oil and natural gas sector (including assets held by Petrobras, now profitable again). Rousseff, who is deepening attention to and relations with other Mercosul (Southern Common Market) countries (Argentina, Paraguay, and Uruguay), may enhance engagement with Argentina and Bolivia to pursue more consistent supply from the neighborhood. This is an example of how Rousseff's prioritization of South American integration, albeit bound to encounter obstacles, serves her diplomatic and domestic growth agenda. Future gas production from the pre-salt formation will greatly reduce Brazil's reliance on Bolivia and may allow Brazil to export gas as liquefied natural gas. In the near term, however, and until pre-salt gas production comes online, Brazil will increase its imports of natural gas.

ELECTRICITY

Brazilian demand for electricity, driven by increasing electrification, industrialization, and a growing middle class able to afford household electronics, is expected to grow by 50 percent over the next decade. This rapid demand growth maintains constant pressure on the system to add new generation capacity.

Hydropower currently accounts for 75 percent of current installed capacity and as much as 85 percent of generation.[21] Though a number of large hydro projects are planned or under construction, hydro's share of power generation is declining. Brazil has already developed roughly half of its economically viable hydropower potential, causing most new sites to be increasingly distant from the large demand centers in the southeast. In addition, many of the most technically attractive sites are located in environmentally sensitive areas, such as the Amazon, which draws opposition from indigenous and environmental groups, complicates the environmental licensing process, and often delays construction.

Because of these difficulties, Brazil will likely pursue more small- and medium-scale projects—those generating fifty megawatts or less, which Brazilians call micro-hydro—and is expected to rely increasingly on natural gas for its incremental electricity needs.

Brazil's reliance on hydropower may also make it vulnerable to climatic shifts in rainfall.[22] Rainfall extremes—both droughts and floods—are expected to become more exaggerated throughout Brazil, making water storage and flow management capability more valuable. Paradoxically, such measures in response to climate change are at odds with the trend toward smaller reservoirs, which are themselves intended to limit the environmental footprint of new hydropower developments.

Greater fuel diversification, particularly greater use of nuclear power or natural-gas-fired generation, has been promoted to reduce Brazil's exposure to drought-induced reductions in hydro availability, which was a primary cause of Brazil's deep power shortage and rationing between 2001 and 2002. Renewable energy technologies, particularly wind and biomass, are supported through specific subsidies as well as special auctions for contracts with power distributors. Brazil is revitalizing its nuclear industry, with the ultimate goal of sourcing all enriched uranium domestically.

In addition to supplying electricity for domestic consumption, Brazil intends to explore, exploit, and enrich uranium for export (a right provided for in the Nuclear Nonproliferation Treaty, of which Brazil is a signatory). The government has resumed construction of a third nuclear power plant, is planning four additional plants over the next twenty years, and is expanding its uranium enrichment facilities. Recently, however, Brazil's turn to nuclear power has come under increasing domestic scrutiny after the devastating effects of the March 2011 earthquake and tsunami on Japan's nuclear reactors.

Conclusions

The Task Force finds that, although Brazil currently has one of the highest shares of renewable energy in power generation in the world, this share will be steadily eroded by continued demand growth, environmental challenges to large hydro projects, and the desire for greater fuel diversity. Areas of mutual interest with the United States include hydropower development and repowering, expanding and strengthening long-distance transmission capacity, the development and deployment of smart grid technologies and processes, and managing greater natural gas use (albeit through different technologies) in an environmentally sensitive way.

ETHANOL

Sugar ethanol has played an important role in Brazil's energy sector since the energy crisis of the 1970s. Brazil is a major global ethanol producer, consumer, and exporter, and plans to double biofuels production over the next decade. Increased production will primarily satisfy domestic demand, though exports are expected to triple to 180,000 barrels per day by 2020. Total ethanol production is now in excess of 430,000 barrels per day, roughly 80 percent of which serves the domestic market. The development of flex-fuel vehicles, which are able to run on any mixture of ethanol and gasoline, in the early 2000s greatly increased ethanol's popularity with consumers.[23]

Brazil's ethanol industry is consolidating as small producers are absorbed and major energy actors such as Petrobras and Shell enter the industry. Logistical constraints, particularly in transporting ethanol from local producers to major markets, have slowed the pace of development in recent years. Several pipeline projects are now under development to relieve the bottlenecks. In addition, concerns about labor conditions and the potential for expanded sugarcane cultivation to push other agricultural activity into the Amazon region have raised sustainability questions.

To meet future biofuel mandates, the United States will likely have to increase its biofuel imports from Brazil. With the U.S. ethanol industry now showing support for phasing out ethanol tariffs in exchange for long-term production credits and infrastructure incentives, American policymakers could use this as an opening within the U.S.-Brazil relationship. American budget hawks see the elimination of the tariffs (at fifty-four cents per gallon on imported ethanol) as a quick win, and industry supporters are increasingly open to greater imports as it becomes clear that meeting future biofuel targets without them will be impossible.

Conclusions and Recommendations

Brazil and the United States are the dominant countries in ethanol production and consumption; their combined 89 percent share of the global ethanol market offers significant opportunities for cooperation. Many bilateral programs have focused on jointly developing related technology and establishing standards and international structures to promote a global ethanol market.

Even as Brazil and the United States work to develop biofuels production capacity in third countries, protectionist U.S. policy toward imported sugar ethanol remains a barrier to developing a global free market for ethanol. The Task Force recommends that the Obama administration make the case in the U.S. Congress for tariff and subsidy reductions or eliminations as smart trade, clean energy, and strategic foreign policies.

Understanding the contentious U.S. political environment, the Task Force encourages Congress to include an elimination of the ethanol tariff in any reform to the ethanol and biofuel tax credit regime. The Task Force recommends that the United States use the proposed tariff elimination to negotiate reductions in barriers for U.S. goods to Brazil. This mutual reduction of tariffs in the name of climate change mitigation could then be promoted as a model for similar agreements between other countries and serve to allay fears that climate-related criteria could be used to increase trade barriers in developing countries. In the interim, the United States can take steps to facilitate a larger integrated ethanol market by cooperating with Brazilians to align biofuels standards.

CLIMATE CHANGE

Brazil's economic success has brought both environmental benefits and challenges. Rising living standards have made environmental protection more of a priority for both the public and the government. At the same time, however, economic growth has brought higher consumption of goods and energy, as well as greater changes in land use to support agricultural expansion.

Brazil's continued economic rise will increase threats to its environment even as its economic wherewithal to address those threats grows. For example, Brazil's growing electricity demand drives greater use of natural-gas-fired power generation and a growing automobile fleet increases gasoline and diesel demand. Development of the pre-salt oil resources risks acute environmental damage as well, as a major accident could damage Brazil's "blue Amazon." Deforestation of the Amazon rainforest, though generally on the decline, remains a major challenge and the primary source of greenhouse gas (GHG) emissions in Brazil.

Conclusions
The Rousseff administration's efforts to mitigate GHG emissions and international efforts to strengthen global commitments to combat climate change will likely come second to Brazil's higher priorities of economic growth and social development. Nevertheless, many areas of climate change mitigation are of mutual interest to Brazil and the United States, opening significant opportunities for cooperation.

BRAZIL'S ENVIRONMENTAL PROFILE

Brazil's relatively green energy sector is recognized as an innovator in environmentally friendly economic development. In fact, GHG emissions from energy use and industrial processes—sectors that are responsible for the majority of emissions worldwide—account for only 20 percent of Brazil's total emissions.

As home to 60 percent of the Amazon rainforest—an area equal in size to the entire European Union—as well as the Cerrado plains and Pantanal wetlands, Brazil hosts flora and fauna that are among the world's most extensive and diverse. Though the Amazon is a major carbon sink and regulator of the global climate, it is also highly susceptible to temperature changes. Current climate models disagree about the impact of rising temperatures on the seasonality and volume of rainfall in this complex ecosystem. However, most predict greater extremes in periodic droughts and floods, and some suggest that even moderate temperature increases could result in a large-scale die-back of the jungle, with profound consequences for rainfall patterns and carbon cycles across the continent and globe.

The Amazon's importance in mitigating climate change and its vulnerability to rising temperatures make forestry management a dominant issue in Brazil's domestic climate change policymaking and its position in international negotiations. Indeed, deforestation in the Amazon alone accounted for 45 percent of the country's total GHG emissions in 2005. Agricultural expansion drives much of the land-use changes, and agriculture and livestock land use, from subsistence farmers to international agribusiness, together form the second-largest source of GHG emissions in Brazil.

BRAZIL'S CLIMATE CHANGE MITIGATION EFFORTS

Climate change has become increasingly important to the Brazilian people, driven by rising per capita income and growing awareness of the issue. Recent polls indicate that roughly 50 percent of Brazilians consider the environment to be their greatest concern, and 90 percent judge global climate change to be a serious problem—nearly double the number of Americans who hold a similar view. The Brazilian government's expanding effort to reduce GHG emissions reflects this rising public awareness.

Previous government programs that helped create Brazil's current low-carbon economy, including the Pro-alcool program that supports ethanol and large-scale hydropower plants, were foremost economic development projects, with the resulting environmental benefits of secondary concern. Similar dual-benefit programs continue, such as dedicated auctions for renewable power generation capacity and energy efficiency programs like Procel and Reluz (electricity) and Conpet (natural gas and petroleum).

More directly focused on climate change, the Brazilian government has implemented policies to limit deforestation under an umbrella Action Plan for the Prevention and Control of Deforestation in the Legal Amazon. It has also created extensive land- and space-based monitoring systems and established large areas protected from economic development.[24] Brazil has also implemented innovative programs to reconcile rural poverty and land clearing, such as the Bolsa Floresta (Forest Grant), which makes conditional cash payments related to forest preservation and is modeled on the highly successful Bolsa Familia program.[25]

In 2010, following the Copenhagen Accord, Brazil submitted to the UN Framework Convention on Climate Change (UNFCCC) a voluntary emissions-reduction plan codified in Brazilian law through the establishment of a National Policy on Climate Change. This plan proposes to reduce Brazil's business as usual (BAU) emissions by some 36 to 39 percent, or roughly one billion metric tons of carbon dioxide (CO_2) equivalency, by 2020 in eleven targets areas.[26]

Reducing deforestation in the Amazon and the Cerrado alone is expected to account for more than 60 percent of the proposed reductions.[27] Agricultural programs are expected to provide 14 to 16 percent and energy-related programs a further 17 to 20 percent. If fully implemented, the plan would reduce Brazil's GHG emissions to roughly 1.7 billion metric tons, or almost 10 percent below the 2005 reported emissions. To put these figures in perspective, these reductions imply that 2020 GHG emissions per unit of GDP would be roughly 47 percent lower than in 2005, assuming that Brazil's average economic growth over the next decade is the same as the most recent historical average.

Conclusions

Despite Brazil's goals, mitigating climate change often conflicts with other governmental priorities, such as poverty reduction, economic development, and expansion of trade. Reducing Amazon deforestation competes with large-scale hydropower development and construction of transcontinental highways to link Brazil's hinterland with the Pacific Ocean. Reductions in land-use and agricultural emissions compete with Brazil's growing agricultural sector. Even the proposed reduction plans have limited capacity and can offset each other—expanding biofuels and hydropower may result in greater land-use emissions. The Task Force warns that these conflicts can reduce the effectiveness of GHG reduction programs and put their sustainability at risk.

The Task Force welcomes Brazil's aggressive position toward reducing domestic GHG emissions, going materially beyond its obligations under current climate agreements. Achieving these goals, however, will be complicated by multiple competing priorities of economic growth, social development, and trade.

INTERNATIONAL IMPLICATIONS

Brazil's green credentials—particularly its recent successes in reducing deforestation in the Amazon, its low-carbon energy sector, and its voluntary plan to dramatically reduce emissions by 2020 despite the upward pressure on emissions that comes from rapid economic growth—and its position as a leading developing economy give it a credible platform to mediate between developing and developed countries.

Brazil shares strategic interests with many diverse countries, making it a natural bridge between many negotiating blocs and an active participant in global climate negotiations. Indeed, Brazil has long played an active role in this arena. The 1992 UN Conference on Environment and Development was held in Rio de Janeiro, and Brazil was the first signatory of the resulting UNFCCC.

Brazil's stance on deforestation programs has shifted significantly in recent years, moving from being a major impediment to the inclusion of forestry programs in the global climate debate to proposing its own detailed plan to manage the Amazon at the Bali conference in 2007. Brazil's growing confidence and greater willingness to propose its own agenda has translated into a higher profile in climate change negotiations. As a member of the BASIC negotiating bloc, which also includes South Africa, India, and China, Brazil played a more prominent role in the negotiations at Copenhagen (COP-15) and Cancún (COP-16). This was most notable in Cancún, where Brazil helped manage the Bolivian delegation's concerns to ensure that these did not derail the wider debate.

As a non–Annex I signatory of the Kyoto Protocol, Brazil has been a major participant in the Clean Development Mechanism (CDM).[28] Brazil is host to the third-largest number of CDM projects: 100 registered projects and 350 more in the accreditation pipeline—together roughly 7 percent of the global total. These projects are, by definition, discrete and measureable projects that reduce carbon emissions from a projected BAU outlook. Brazil's projects focus almost exclusively on the energy sector—primarily biomass cogeneration, small hydro, wind, and fuel switching—although five of the registered projects, totaling 12 percent of expected emissions reductions, center on capturing methane emissions from landfill waste.[29]

Nonetheless, like many developing economies, Brazil is wary of international programs—particularly those related to land use and the Amazon—that may infringe upon its sovereignty or constrain its economic growth. Brazil has also criticized project-oriented programs such as CDM and Reducing Emissions from Deforestation and Forest Degradation (UN-REDD), arguing that a more wide-ranging approach is needed to avoid carbon leakage (displacement of carbon-emitting activities rather than a true reduction of them).

Under the Rousseff administration, Brazil's commitment to combating climate change is expected to continue, albeit in the context of a firm focus on economic growth. Rousseff is quite familiar with climate change issues, having formerly been the minister of mines and energy and the leader of Brazil's delegation to COP-15. Her inauguration speech directly addressed Brazil's obligation to prove that economic growth can be environmentally sustainable.

Conclusions and Recommendations

The Task Force recognizes that, like all of Rousseff's initiatives, climate change goals will be linked to domestic growth priorities. Internationally, Brazil will likely continue to position itself as an intermediary between developed and developing nations—acting as an example to developing countries of how sustainable development can be achieved and maintaining the need for differentiated responsibilities and greater reduction efforts from developed countries.

Agreement on the path of the UNFCCC process is unlikely in the near term because Brazil wants a legally binding agreement and the United

States will not pursue one. Still, the Task Force urges both the United States and Brazil to continue the constructive and pragmatic approach outlined at the 2010 Cancún summit by beginning to implement the adaptation, mitigation, transparency, technology, and financing steps shaped by the summit's parties. The Task Force also encourages Brazil and the United States to focus on bilateral climate change mitigation efforts, which offer ample opportunity for cooperation, especially with respect to agriculture and land use, forestry, and subnational cooperation between states and regions.

The Task Force recognizes that the importance and complexity of the Amazon suggest it should be managed comprehensively, coordinating all relevant parties to help preserve it from climate change, deforestation, and fire. As a steward of the largest share of the Amazon and as the largest economy in the region, Brazil has a natural role in leading cooperation across cultures, political jurisdictions, research disciplines, and industries. The Task Force recommends the United States, where possible, use its voice in international financial institutions and other multilateral settings to help mobilize resources that can support Brazil's coordination.

There is ample scope for the United States and Brazil to work together to improve climate modeling and data gathering capabilities, particularly in the Amazon region. Current climate forecasting models inadequately model the potential consequences of climate change on the Amazon rainforest and other Brazilian ecosystems. Brazil has established a number of international research groups and programs to improve global understanding of the Amazon, its role in regulating the global climate, and its vulnerability to climate change.

The Task Force encourages greater U.S. support for and collaboration with Brazil's programs that monitor deforestation and climate change, which advance understanding of Brazil's complex ecosystems and improve the utility of global climate models in general. These programs include: the Large-scale Biosphere-Atmosphere Experiment in Amazonia, a program focused on understanding the role of the Amazon in global environmental change; the National Institute for Space Research's (INPE) various real-time space- and land-based deforestation monitoring systems; regional and global climate models being jointly developed by Brazil and South Africa; and the Prediction and Research Moored Array in the Tropical Atlantic, which studies ocean-atmosphere interactions. These bilateral efforts would help further Brazil's space-related science and technology ambitions while addressing deforestation and climate change and the relationship between them. The U.S.-Brazil biofuels memorandum of understanding (MOU) is a good example of both countries jointly promoting the adoption of climate-friendly technologies in third countries, though execution could be strengthened. The Task Force encourages the development of similar efforts to reduce deforestation, such as the Bolsa Floresta conservation program, in third-party countries.

Brazil as a Regional and Global Diplomat

Because Brazil's presence is now felt globally, long-standing powers—the United States in particular—are grappling with how to perceive, predict, and work in concert (where and when appropriate) with Brazil. As a nonpermanent member of the UNSC from 2010 through 2011, Brazil has engaged in debates on the world's most pressing security issues, including Libya, the Israeli-Palestinian conflict, and nuclear disarmament and nonproliferation generally and with respect to Iran.

To increase the influence of nontraditional powers and advance a South-South agenda, Brazil joined with Russia, India, and China to create the BRIC forum. The BRICS group—which, as of 2011, includes South Africa—held its first formal summit in 2009 to respond to the global financial crisis and has since focused primarily on economic coordination.[30]

Brazil has also operated within the IBSA forum, established by India, Brazil, and South Africa in 2003 to strengthen economic partnerships between them and coordinate efforts on world trade negotiations and UNSC expansion. Likewise, Brazil has worked with the other BASIC countries to organize common positions going into UN climate change conferences.

Brazilian peacekeepers, under the auspices of the UN, are stationed across the world, especially in lusophone Africa and in Haiti, where Brazil has led the UN Stabilization Mission in Haiti (MINUSTAH) since 2004 and made among the earliest and largest financial contributions there since the 2010 earthquake. Brazilian multinational corporations operate and invest across Asia, Africa, Europe, and North and South America. Brazil also plays a leading role within longstanding and newly formed regional institutions (such as the Union of South American Nations and the Community of Latin American and Caribbean States), most of which eschew U.S. membership in order to foster a South American or Latin American identity.

Brazil has historically benefitted from working within existing global governance institutions and regimes. Therefore Brazil seeks not to upend these institutions but to adapt and employ them as platforms to advance Brazilian interests. Brazil encourages reform that would restructure these organizations to more accurately reflect and advance an emerging multipolar order. In this vein, Brazil has long argued for better representation for emerging and developing nations in the UN, World Bank, IMF, and WTO.

THE UNITED NATIONS

Brazil has a long history of frustrated attempts to gain a seat at the global high table at the United Nations.[31] Movement toward Security Council reform was reenergized in 2010 with the start of new text-based intergovernmental negotiations, but the overhaul remains a distant prospect.

Beginning in the early 1990s, Germany, Japan, and India joined Brazil to form the Group of Four (G4) in a concerted effort to join the UNSC as permanent members. The G4 advocates for six additional permanent seats—two each from Asia and Africa and one each from Latin America and Europe—and four nonpermanent ones. In an effort to compromise, the G4 would accept new permanent seats without a veto.

Arguing that the UNSC represents an outdated postwar international order, both Brazil and Germany have reasoned that their membership in an expanded UNSC would increase the body's legitimacy and thus its effectiveness. Brazil bases its case for a seat also on being South America's largest country in terms of territory, population, and economy. Notably, although Mexico, Venezuela, Argentina, and Colombia have, at various times, contested Brazil's readiness to represent the region, neither the current permanent members nor the members of the G4 contend that UNSC membership is grounded exclusively in geographic representation.

Brazil and its allies within the IBSA forum also stress the need to expand the permanent and nonpermanent membership of the UNSC. Brazil counts on backing from other partners as well. In 2010, the Community of Portuguese Language Countries—which includes Portugal, Brazil, Angola, Cape Verde, Guinea-Bissau, Mozambique, São Tomé and Príncipe, and East Timor—affirmed their support for Brazil's bid for a UNSC permanent seat. Major powers such as the United Kingdom, France, and Russia likewise support Brazil's inclusion.

Brazil's participation in UN peacekeeping missions has also bolstered its case for permanent UNSC membership. Brazilians have participated in over twenty UN peacekeeping operations since 1985. Under UN auspices, Brazil has sent troops or observers to lusophone Africa in particular, including Angola and Mozambique, and is now working with the UN Office on Drugs and Crime to build a police training academy in Guinea-Bissau. As a nonpermanent UNSC member during the 1990s, Brazil did not vote in favor of peacekeeping missions in Haiti. Over the next several years, however, Brazil's foreign policy establishment increasingly warmed to working with and within multilateral institutions. In 2004, Brazil volunteered to lead MINUSTAH. Brazil responded to the January 2010 Haitian earthquake with increased financial and personnel support in Haiti, reaffirming its commitment to Haiti's development and to UN peacekeeping.

Generally, though, the Task Force finds that Brazilian contributions to the UN could be expanded: Brazil ranks fourteenth among UN troop contributors, behind its much smaller neighbor Uruguay and trailing India and Nigeria, among others; it also provides less than 1 percent of the UN's regular budget—and only 0.2 percent of the peacekeeping budget.

Brazil's divergence from the P5 to negotiate a nuclear swap deal with Iran and Turkey in 2010, followed by Brazil's vote against the P5-supported round of sanctions, directly contradicts the U.S. strategic objective of containing Iran's nuclear ambitions. Brazil is nevertheless fully implementing the sanctions and it appears that the United States has left the door open for Brazil's eventual permanent UNSC membership. In a joint press conference with the Brazilian foreign minister in February 2011 ahead of Obama's trip, Secretary of State Hillary Rodham Clinton remarked, "We very much admire Brazil's growing global leadership and its aspiration to be a permanent member of the United Nations Security Council. We look forward to a constructive dialogue with Brazil on this issue during President Obama's trip and going forward. We believe that there are many, many areas of leadership multilaterally that Brazil will be demonstrating, and we want to support those efforts."

While in Brasília, Obama stopped short of endorsing Brazil, but rather affirmed the general disposition to "make sure that the new

realities of the twenty-first century are reflected in international institutions . . . including the United Nations, where Brazil aspires to a seat on
the Security Council."[32] Obama's 2010 endorsement of India as a permanent member of the Security Council bodes well for Brazil generally, in the sense that U.S. support for UNSC reform is marked. Unlike
India, Brazil renounced its military nuclear program decades ago and
signed on to the Nuclear Nonproliferation Treaty. Endorsing Brazil
would send a strong signal that those who abide by the rules of multilateral treaties and institutions are to be rewarded.

Conclusions and Recommendations

The Task Force welcomes President Obama and Secretary Clinton's
encouragement of and openness to discuss Brazil's pursuit of a permanent seat on the UN Security Council. But the Task Force recommends
that the Obama administration now fully endorse Brazil's permanent
UNSC membership. The Task Force believes that Brazil's prospec-
tive permanent membership on the UNSC would compel it toward
increased responsibility and accountability on a host of global issues.
The Task Force encourages the administration to address important
regional, diplomatic, multilateral, and global governance dimensions
of such a step as it engages Brazil in an intense dialogue on this matter.

The 2010 U.S. National Security Strategy acknowledged that the
"international architecture of the 20th century is buckling" and Obama
already has backed UNSC reform and expansion, arguing in India that
a "just and sustainable international order" includes "a United Nations
that is efficient, effective, credible, and legitimate." The Task Force
agrees that an expanded UNSC is in the interest of the United States.
In this light, an endorsement of Brazil as a permanent member of the
UNSC comes not at the expense of Germany, Japan, or India (Brazil's
fellow G4 members), but rather smoothes the path for their accession
as well.

A formal endorsement from the United States for Brazil would go far
to overcome lingering suspicion within the Brazilian government that
the U.S. commitment to a mature relationship between equals is largely
rhetorical. With reform years away, there is little to lose and much to
gain from official U.S. support for a permanent Brazilian seat now.

With Brazil as a permanent UNSC member, Brazil and the United
States would necessarily work together on all major international
security, development, and humanitarian challenges going forward,

potentially creating the conditions for closer U.S.-Brazil relations and cooperation across an even wider range of issues, including within the region. For the United States, building a Brazil strategy is not a zero-sum game with respect to U.S. ties in Latin America. Indeed, the Task Force encourages the United States to develop a robust bilateral, regional, and global affairs dialogue with the other countries of Latin America.

Discussion of this important issue should include an extensive review of possible repercussions, including the impact on U.S. relationships in the region, such as with Canada and Mexico. Even as the rationale for a Brazilian seat on a reformed UNSC extends well beyond regional criteria, the Task Force urges Brazil, with responsibility as a pivotal power in the region and globally, to take account of Latin American views of global issues.

ABSTENTIONS

In general, Brazil is deferential to self-determination and sovereignty and will likely maintain its pattern of frequent abstention at the UN. The Task Force advises U.S. policymakers to understand that Brazil's abstention does not necessarily reflect disagreement with the thrust of a resolution. Rather, Brazilians use the abstention to express frustration with unsystematic treatment of issues, often raising, for example, the contradiction of the international community's censuring of Iran but not of Saudi Arabia. In Brazilian foreign policy, explanations accompanying abstentions are a way to express concern while upholding insistence on universality.

Abstention with explanations may seem to U.S. policymakers like equivocation. The Task Force encourages U.S. policymakers to regard Brazil's different approach at the UN within the framework of their maturing friendship: mutual interests will not always result in identical action. Brazilians see their abstention as a way of exercising global leadership, not as an abdication of responsibility, and they note that an abstention is not a "no" vote. At the same time, Brazil does not risk losing its independence when it votes with the United States from time to time.

HUMAN RIGHTS

The Task Force is encouraged by President Rousseff's stated commitment to human rights. Rousseff's personal history has placed a spotlight on human rights, and Brazil is lending its voice to advance the many dimensions of and threats to human rights across the world. Rousseff signaled Brazil's coming emphasis on international human rights and a departure from her predecessor when, during her first media interview after her election, she asserted that she would not have abstained on a 2010 UN human rights resolution on Iran.[33] Early in the Rousseff presidency, Brazil has made overtures on human rights issues in Latin America, the Middle East, and Iran, and Rousseff maintained the position of the special secretary for human rights as a cabinet-level position.

The Task Force also notes that Brazil has made a considerable contribution to the improvement of human rights of its citizens in recent years. Brazil's historic transition from a military-led to a democratically elected government has produced economic growth and an opening of society, and that has dramatically reduced poverty and childhood malnutrition by nearly 80 percent.

Presidents Obama and Rousseff can be powerful voices calling for racial, ethnic, and gender equality in their own countries and abroad, having broken barriers as the first African-American president in the United States and the first female president in Brazil. Likewise, both President Rousseff and Secretary Clinton have identified the importance of girls' education and the advancement of women as matters of development and security and can use their bona fides to further elevate this issue both domestically and abroad.

Conclusions and Recommendations

Brazil would strengthen its human rights credentials and influence within the UN Human Rights Council were it to apply universality to itself as assiduously as it demands it from others. For example, the number of extrajudicial executions by police is extremely high: Rio de Janeiro and São Paulo police forces combined kill more than one thousand people each year. Brazil has not yet passed legislation that would establish a truth commission to investigate dictatorship-era human rights abuses. The Task Force welcomes Brazil's voice and positive influence in advancing human rights throughout the Americas and internationally and encourages Brazil and the United States to seek ways to cooperate generally with respect to human rights.

The Task Force encourages both the United States and Brazil to make a pledge of support to the United Nations Entity for Gender Equality and the Empowerment of Women, which was established in

2010 and has received no Brazilian or U.S. government financial contributions to date.

INTERNATIONAL TRADE

Brazil aims to restructure global trade architecture to advance both trade liberalization and more equitable access to markets while also providing a degree of protection to its domestic markets and participants. Brazil, along with India, spearheaded the creation of the G20 developing nations in Cancún in 2003 to strengthen their negotiating power within the WTO. (Brazil's role in the financial G20 is addressed below.)

As a bridge between the developed and developing worlds, Brazil alternately compromises on its commitment to liberalization and its solidarity with developing nations, which, like Brazil itself, are at times inclined toward industrial and farm protectionism. For example, Brazil has supported exceptions from tariff limits for "special products" in developing countries confronted by a surge of imports. On the other hand, in 2008, Brazil broke from Argentina, China, and India to endorse a proposal that would lower the ceiling on U.S. agricultural subsidies in exchange for cuts to industrial tariffs.

The Task Force expects that near-term agreement on the Doha Development Agenda is unlikely; in the meantime, Brazil—within the G20 and independently—will likely continue to balance its free trade interests with its persistent desire to elevate the influence and interests of developing nations within trade negotiations. This duality of interests reflects the duality within Brazil as both a developed and developing country.

Conclusions and Recommendations

The Task Force welcomes the new agreement on trade and economic cooperation and the establishment of a U.S.-Brazil Commission on Economic and Trade Relations, announced during the presidential visit in March 2011.[34] The commission seeks to promote bilateral economic and trade cooperation, including advocating for the removal of trade and investment obstacles, particularly in the regulatory field. Although achieving resolutions on issues of subsidies and market access will remain difficult, the Task Force encourages trade discussions within the yearly framework established. The U.S. trade representative and Brazilian counterparts should focus first on less controversial issues on which interests are aligned, such as trade facilitation and customs modernization. The Task Force also calls on both countries to step away from protectionist practices and subsidies and to embrace a more open trade architecture.

The settlement of the U.S.-Brazil cotton dispute in 2010 (which avoided WTO-authorized Brazilian retaliation for U.S. subsidies) was based on the premise that the Obama administration would work with the U.S. Congress to bring its agricultural subsidy regime into compliance with WTO norms in the next farm bill in 2012. The Task Force applauds this step and encourages implementation.

GLOBAL FINANCIAL ARCHITECTURE

Formally known as the Group of Twenty Finance Ministers and Central Bank Governors, the G20 aims to give greater representation to emerging economies that did not belong to, and whose interests were therefore not represented directly by, the G8.[35] At the height of the financial crisis, Brazil sought to solidify its leadership and credibility in the G20 by making a $10 billion one-off contribution to the IMF. Given the G20's inherent emphasis on developing but underrepresented economies, Brazil is a natural leader within the group. Brazil has worked within the G20 to advance its protracted efforts to increase voting rights for emerging economies within the IMF and World Bank, and a number of reforms have increased Brazil's voting power.[36]

Brazil will likely continue its efforts toward restructuring the architecture of global institutions and regimes so that they better reflect the emergence of nontraditional powers. Brazil has already proven successful at increasing official voting shares within global financial institutions, though not to the extent it desires. With Brazil's priority—reform of the IMF and World Bank—at least partially addressed, the Task Force expects that Brazil will advocate against protectionist measures and budget cuts in rich countries, continue to argue for stricter government oversight mechanisms and balancing of financial markets, and emphasize avoiding what it considers the manipulation—especially the artificially low valuations—of U.S. and Chinese currencies.

Conclusions and Recommendations
The Task Force recognizes Brazil's voice in the G20 and Bretton Woods institutions. The Task Force notes that ceding space to emerging

powers in the Bretton Woods institutions ultimately strengthens global institutions. The Task Force welcomes U.S. support for the opening of membership in important international bodies such as the Financial Stability Board (FSB) to G20 members, including Brazil, as well as U.S. support for changes in quotas and shares in the IMF and World Bank, and the Task Force recognizes Brazil's constructive role in advocating these changes.

Moving forward, the Task Force sees a positive agenda for the United States and Brazil in the G20, the international financial institutions, the FSB, and other international bodies dealing with financial and monetary affairs such as financial regulatory reform, global imbalances, currency policy, the availability of credit in both recovering and developing economies, combating money laundering, and a development agenda that builds on Brazil's strong experience with conditional cash transfers.

BRAZIL AND ITS REGION

By far the largest country in South America—in terms of land mass, population, and economy—Brazil borders ten of the continent's twelve other countries. One of the last countries in South America to transition from a monarchy and to abolish slavery, Brazil did not experience a convulsive anticolonial revolution (against, in its case, the Portuguese crown). With an atypical history and different identity from its neighbors, Brazil hesitates to characterize itself as Latin American, emphasizing instead its status as a South American nation. At the same time, the region is often reluctant to accept the Portuguese-speaking giant as one of its own. Growing interdependence between Brazil and its neighbors further complicates the distinctions and asymmetries, which are reflected in relationships at once characterized by ambivalence, indifference, tension, and deference.

Brazil is escalating investment and trade throughout the region. The growing Brazilian economy depends on further infrastructure and energy integration across the continent. Given Brazil's nine-thousand-mile border and its own rising drug consumption and export problems, the country has a mounting interest in working with its neighbors to address transnational illegal traffic of drugs, people, and counterfeit goods. Brazilians are increasing their physical presence in South

America as well: for example, more than thirty thousand Brazilians reside in Bolivia and control as much as 40 percent of Bolivia's soybean production.[37] Brazilians are also buying up farmland across the Paraguayan border; the tens of thousands of Brazilians in Paraguay have come to be known as *Brasiguayos.*

Brazil encourages greater cooperation in South America within organizations like Mercosul and Unasul, under cautious Brazilian leadership designed to be as free of friction as possible. Indeed, Brazilian officials actively shirk the label of regional leader so as not to antagonize its neighbors and to maintain good relations in the region. The rest of South America depends increasingly on trade with and investment from Brazil. But Brazil's smaller neighbors worry about depending too heavily on Brazil—economically and as a global interlocutor for the region. Some South Americans are wary that Brazil, a new potential hegemon with its sights set on global power, may not have the region's interests at heart.

Brazil is proud of a long tradition of nonintervention in the internal affairs of its neighbors. But as Brazil has looked to exercise its power and influence beyond the region, it is legitimate to ask what role Brazil strives to play closer to home, beyond the economic sphere. Mindful of its own history of military rule, Brazil has acted to repudiate military coups in the region: Paraguay in 1996, Ecuador in 2000, and Honduras in 2009. However, Brazil has been less vocal on issues of democratic erosion, preferring quiet diplomacy to public condemnation, or alleging that questionable conduct is a matter of sovereign authority or to be addressed multilaterally. President Rousseff, who was arrested and tortured by the military regime for her underground activities, has the potential to be a powerful voice for human rights and democratic values in Latin America, helping ensure that its neighborhood is populated with stable democracies that will in turn bolster Brazil's economic positioning.

Conclusions and Recommendations

The Task Force finds that as Brazil increasingly roots itself in South America to advance its domestic and global agenda, the United States would benefit from identifying spaces where the United States and Brazil can work together to advance mutual goals. The Task Force believes, therefore, that it is in the interest of the United States to understand the Brazilian regional project and welcome Brazil's leadership in the hemisphere, especially when it advances shared values of inclusiveness, development, democracy, and human rights.

All countries in the Americas are adjusting to Brazil's rise; U.S. efforts to do so do not reflect a decrease in the importance of its other relationships in Latin America but rather a recognition that the United States has a clear national interest in solidifying a mature, and heretofore inadequately developed, relationship with Brazil.

Brazil engages in the collective defense of democracy by condemning and working to preempt traditional military coups. It does not, however, engage in what U.S. policymakers would recognize as democracy or human rights promotion. For example, though the current Brazilian government does not endorse Venezuelan president Hugo Chávez's abuses of executive power and human rights, it makes no visible efforts to encourage him to cease those activities. Instead, Brazil has chosen to lead by the example of its own democratic bona fides and successful social policies. Brazil's greater diplomatic role in the Andes and within South American multilateral institutions has provided a different approach to that of Venezuela. Brazil's diplomacy has helped neutralize Chávez's ideological resonance in the region, albeit not through the type of public censure that is more familiar to the United States.

The Task Force encourages the United States to continue to deepen a dialogue with Brazil over opportunities to use their different approaches and strengths to encourage strong democratic institutions and practices throughout the region. Both countries should collaborate to find collective approaches to strengthen democracy in the region.

BRAZIL'S TRADE RELATIONSHIPS IN THE REGION

Though Brazil has emerged as an engine of regional growth, the asymmetry of Brazil's trade relationships along with its protectionist practices make Brazil the target of resentment as well. The Brazilian economy remains relatively closed: trade makes up about 25 percent of Brazilian GDP, which amounts to about 50 percent of Argentina's ratio and less than 33 percent of Chile's ratio. In fact, throughout the 1990s and 2000s, Brazil prioritized the weaker trade bloc of Mercosul over the U.S.-backed Free Trade Area of the Americas (FTAA). In addition to the benefits of the less open Mercosul, Brazil assessed that reducing its barriers to trade—which had significant domestic political implications—would not be met with reciprocal steps by the United States, particularly in the critical agricultural sector.

However, Brazilians see regional asymmetries as a potential obstacle to their objective of a peaceful and stable South America. Brazil's interest in reducing these imbalances may mean that Rousseff will strengthen Mercosul in order to bolster regional stability, develop infrastructure that benefits Brazilian and South American industry, ensure more reliable access to resources (particularly natural gas), and establish South America as Brazil's strategic anchor for its global agenda. A stronger South American common market and customs union would bolster the continent's image as a cohesive and internationally relevant trade bloc and improve Brazil's negotiating position with respect to developed countries and their trade blocs.

Cognizant of Venezuela's weak adhesion to Mercosul's democratic charter, the Lula administration nonetheless supported Venezuela's controversial accession into Mercosul on the basis of potential commercial and economic gains. The inclusion of Venezuela may reflect a judgment by Brazil and other full members of Mercosul that integrating it advances the region's trade goals and brings Venezuela "inside the tent," thereby facilitating conversation and negotiation and diffusing Venezuela's attentions away from potential conflict in the Andean region.

Brazil has negotiated trade agreements with all but two of its neighbors (Guyana and Suriname) and continues to deepen trade relationships in the region. For example, in 2010, bilateral trade with Argentina—Brazil's largest trade partner in Latin America—rose to a record $32.95 billion (up from the previous record of $30.864 billion in 2008). As a whole, Brazil's trade with Latin American countries exceeds flows between Brazil and China and Brazil and the United States (though no single country in the region outpaces Brazil's bilateral trade with either).

Colombia under President Juan Manuel Santos has been arguably the most assertive in its efforts to deepen and balance trade with Brazil.[38] Brazil, as a sign of its expanded outreach to the northern part of the continent, has likewise turned to Colombia as an attractive destination for Brazilian investment. While Brazil has encouraged bilateral diplomacy between presidents Santos and Chávez, it has also benefitted economically from tensions between Colombia and Venezuela: Brazilian exports to Venezuela have substituted for traditional exporters in Colombia, making Venezuela even more dependent on Brazilian goods.

Although Bolivia's 2006 expropriation of Petrobras's natural gas operations strained Bolivia's relationship with Brazil, Petrobras continues to administer the extraction activities and is today the single largest taxpayer in Bolivia.[39] Indeed, Brazilian bilateral and multilateral diplomacy and counternarcotics assistance in Bolivia are examples of a strategy of engagement that has helped advance Brazilian economic and security interests as well as regional stability.

Brazil has a surprisingly small trade relationship with Mexico—Latin America's second-largest economy—amounting to about $7 billion in 2010. Mexico and Brazil are now negotiating a free trade agreement. To be sure, Brazil will compete not just with the United States but also with China for the Mexican market. Notably, since 2008, Brazilian sales to Mexico have tripled, whereas those from China have multiplied twenty-fold. Still, Mexico's turn south reflects a growing tendency for Latin American countries to look to Brazil to boost growth.

Brazil has a unique opportunity to show leadership on issues of trade, not only within Mercosul and with neighboring associate members, but broadly in the Western Hemisphere as well.[40] Brazil's significant economic progress since the failed FTAA discussions puts it in a position to help lead a revival of hemisphere-wide negotiations and to do so from a position of strength.

BRAZIL'S INVESTMENT RELATIONSHIPS IN THE REGION

Latin Americans tend to view Brazil's outward FDI and Brazilian projects in the region with mixed feelings. Overt nationalism often goes hand in hand with Brazilian investment. At the same time, Brazil's investments are important to many Latin American economies.[41] In 2009, BNDES extended a record $8.3 billion in credit for projects outside Brazil. In 2010, overall BNDES disbursements reached more than $100 billion, up 23 percent from 2009, exceeding both those of the Inter-American Development Bank and the World Bank.

Brazilian investment can also bring welcome expertise. Between 2010 and 2014, Petrobras—with its reputation for world-class deepwater exploration and extraction—has committed $400 million to develop Colombia's underwater oil reserves. Odebrecht, a Brazilian construction company, with financing from BNDES, is investing upward of $400 million to renovate Cuba's port of Mariel, which will increase

Brazil's commercial and investment presence in the Gulf of Mexico and the Caribbean Basin.

Latin American nations need and welcome, though at times resent, Brazil's active role in their economies.[42] Trade imbalances and Brazil's ability to invest heavily abroad only underscore the asymmetry that defines Brazilian relations with the neighborhood. Brazil therefore seeks to tread lightly in the region. Rarely do Brazilian officials refer to a coordinated strategy of investment in South America, trying to avoid the reputation of an exploitative hegemon. With significant leadership from Rousseff during her leadership of the Casa Civil, Lula's government deliberately carried out an unprecedented consolidation and capitalization of Brazil's national champions—Braskem, Vale, Bunge, JBS, and Petrobras, to name a few—to encourage their increased internationalization and competitiveness in Latin America and throughout the world.

Conclusions

The Task Force finds that Brazil will deepen its economic relationships with South America while aiming to minimize conflict and negative reactions to its growing financial and physical presence. However, as Brazil's profile continues to rise, it will likely encounter expectations for greater market openness, transparency, and public financing for non-Brazilian entities and will have to address these expectations.

MULTILATERAL ORGANIZATIONS

Brazil's regional and global ambitions are not mutually exclusive. Mercosul and Unasul fit into a larger Brazilian endeavor to establish South America—a land mass that has historically lacked a cohesive identity—as an attractive trade bloc and global strategic actor, with Brazil as its anchor.

Rhetorically, at least, Brazil has prioritized regional integration, and it stands at the helm of a number of Latin American multilateral institutions, notably Mercosul, Unasul, and the still largely unarticulated Comunidad de Estados Latinoamericanos y Caribeños (Community of Latin American States, or CELAC). True to form, Brazil tends to play down its leadership role within these still-evolving organizations.

Mercosul includes Argentina, Paraguay, and Uruguay as full members and Bolivia, Chile, Colombia, Ecuador, and Peru as associate members; Venezuela's incorporation as a full member still awaits approval from the Paraguayan congress. Mercosul's revitalization was a stated priority for Lula entering office in 2003; though progress has been slow, full members reached a consensus on the distribution of customs revenue and agreed to eliminate the double charge of the common external tariff in August 2010.

Brazil was instrumental in the 2004 formation of Unasul, which aims to create a single South American market and to foster economic and infrastructure cooperation and development. In 2008, Brazil led the way to form the South American Defense Council as a cooperative security suborganization under Unasul. Unasul serves as an alternative to the OAS and seeks to provide regional solutions to regional problems. At the same time, Unasul, which adopted a democratic charter in 2010 and is generally more focused on political and social issues than Mercosul, balances the Venezuela-dominated Alianza Bolivariana para los Pueblos de Nuestra América (the Bolivarian Alliance for the Peoples of Our America, or ALBA). Unasul has been most effective at ad hoc mediation, diffusing Ecuador's police uprising and Colombia-Venezuela tensions in 2010.

CELAC, founded in 2010, is the descendent of the Rio Group and the Latin American and Caribbean Summit; still in its early stages of formation, CELAC would be the first formal association of states to include every Latin American and Caribbean nation and exclude the United States and Canada. A meeting of CELAC presidents would help elucidate the Rousseff administration's approach to Venezuela, among other countries.

Conclusions and Recommendations

As Brazil deepens its roots in South America and strengthens multilateral institutions like Mercosul and Unasul, the Task Force welcomes Brazil's growing role in South American diplomacy, conflict prevention, peace, and security efforts. The Task Force supports the creation and consolidation of effective regional institutions and understands that Brazil's and the region's emphasis on multilateralism is an intrinsic dimension of their foreign policies, necessary to ensure a stable and peaceful democratic environment. Though the United States is not, nor should it be, a formal member of these subregional institutions, the Task Force encourages the United States to work with Unasul, Mercosul, and eventually CELAC to establish and define channels for communication.

BRAZIL'S RISING ROLE IN AFRICA

Brazil is the latest among the BRICS to make a strategic play to advance its global legitimacy and status through diversified market channels and diplomatic ties in Africa. Under Lula's leadership, Brazil conferred considerable weight to prioritizing Brazil's Africa relations. Framed within Brazil's South-South agenda, Lula made eleven official visits to the continent, traveling to twenty-five countries—more than any other Brazilian president or BRIC head of state. In the first part of this century, Brazil has doubled the number of its embassies in Africa to thirty-four, pushing beyond its traditional sphere of influence in the former Portuguese colonies. Boosting relations within Africa's fifty-three-member bloc at the UN has long carried currency in Brazil's bid for a permanent seat in an expanded Security Council.

With the world's largest population of people of African descent, Brazil is strategically leveraging its deep historical, linguistic, and cultural affiliations to forge economic and political inroads. On several of his visits to the continent, Lula issued apologies for Brazil's role in the African slave trade. Although largely overshadowed by China's high-profile push into Africa, there is now a new level of interconnection between Africa and Brazil, one that the Rousseff administration is intent on deepening.

Trade between Brazil and Africa has grown to approximately $26 billion in 2008, up from just $3 billion in 2001, making Brazil Africa's tenth-largest trading partner. Whereas China's economic footprint is more widespread across the continent, Brazil's activity is largely concentrated in the extractive industries, such as oil and mining, and a few major trading partners: Nigeria, Angola, Algeria, South Africa, and Libya, which together account for 77 percent of Brazil's trade with Africa.

Brazilian multinational companies are steadily acquiring presence in Africa and have been successful in connecting to and involving local communities, making a concerted effort to build capacity. For instance, Odebrecht has operated in Angola since 1975; today it is the largest private-sector employer in the country, with ventures spanning food and ethanol production, offices, factories, and supermarkets. Petrobras and Vale are at the vanguard of Africa's repositioning as the next frontier for the development of natural resources and infrastructure.

In line with its efforts to boost worldwide biofuels demand, Brazil is a pivotal actor in the expansion of biofuels initiatives in Africa. Synergy has been notable between the Brazilian private sector and development agencies like BNDES and ABC (Brazil's USAID equivalent) in promoting biofuels and technology development in Africa. Brazil has drawn upon its expertise in renewable energy to assist Africa in filling its knowledge gap.

African partners also benefit from Brazil's knowledge sharing and technical assistance, particularly with respect to tropical agricultural technology. Brazil has invested more than $4 billion in Africa's agriculture sector over the past five years to develop production capacity. In a landmark agreement, Embrapa opened a satellite regional office in Ghana to deepen research collaboration and strengthen its advisory role throughout the continent.

Through the transfer of technology, skills training, research and development, and the infusion of capital, Brazil is breaking fresh ground in constructing a new development paradigm. For example, the Africa-Brazil Cooperation Programme on Social Protection, launched in 2009, creates a platform for Brazilian experts to work with their African counterparts in facilitating exchange on various social development policies, such as Bolsa Família and HIV/AIDS prevention and treatment initiatives. Brazil is also active within a number of multilateral organizations—the Summit of the Community of Portuguese Speaking Countries, the World Social Forum, the WTO, the IBSA Dialogue Forum, and the Africa-South America Summit—to advocate for sustainable development in Africa.

Conclusions

Africa is likely to remain part of Brazil's global strategic calculus as it seeks greater international influence, natural resources, and an expanded market for its goods—both concrete material products and the Brazilian narrative itself. The Task Force finds that Brazil's increasing involvement in Africa offers an instructive model of democratic governance and economic development.

THE MIDDLE EAST

During his presidency, Lula made a concerted effort to establish Brazil's presence in the Middle East and to welcome regional leaders in Brazil and Latin America generally. Beyond economic justifications ($20 billion of trade between Brazil and Arab nations in 2008) and cultural ties (as many as twelve million Brazilians of Middle Eastern descent), Brazil sees itself as a legitimate actor in the Israeli-Palestinian peace process, which it judges could benefit from new diplomatic voices.

Brazil, South Africa, and India (an unsurprising trio given their efforts for UNSC membership) were the only extraregional, non-Islamic, nontraditional donor countries to participate in the 2007 Annapolis Middle East peace conference. Leaked diplomatic cables have shown that U.S. officials viewed Lula and former foreign minister Celso Amorim's engagement in the Middle East as one-sided (in favor of Palestine) and meddlesome.[43] Lula's efforts to play peacemaker were capped by a series of individual meetings with Palestinian president Mahmoud Abbas and Israeli president Shimon Peres, both of whom visited Brasília in 2009 and seemed to encourage Brazil's participation in negotiations. However, whether Brazil will play a productive role in this conflict is subject to debate in Israel.

In one of Lula's last moves as president, Brazil declared its full recognition of the Palestinian state within the pre-1967 borders. Brazil's announcement sparked a series of other such declarations from the region.

Rousseff's position on some Middle East security issues—condemnation of atrocities in Libya and the vote to approve a special human rights rapporteur for Iran—have signaled differentiation from Lula's strictly noninterventionist approach. Still, Brazil did abstain on the Security Council's vote to authorize intervention in Libya, as did Russia, India, China, and Germany. Brazil's formal vote on a looming UN vote on Palestinian statehood in fall 2011 will be another indication of the extent to which Rousseff will distinguish her foreign policy from her predecessor's with respect to the Middle East.

Conclusions

The Task Force finds that Brazil's engagement in Middle East peace negotiations was consistent with Lula's expansive foreign policy and is likely to evolve as Brazil aims to build international bridges and a constituency to support its bid for UNSC permanent membership. Especially in light of the 2010 Iran episode, the Task Force deems that Brazil's engagement specifically in Middle East security issues may dilute Brazil's credentials to negotiate on other issues of international concern in which its participation is both more logical and more necessary. The Task Force also recognizes that social, political, and diplomatic developments related to the upheaval in the Arab world may be seen by Brazil as an opportunity to continue to deepen Brazilian diplomatic, commercial, and economic ties in the region.

Brazil and the United States

Brazil and the United States have many common interests, but their foreign policies have occasionally diverged—whether on Latin America and the Middle East or on trade and monetary policy. At the same time, the two countries are deepening connectivity in third countries, subnationally, and through their private sectors and civil societies. The United States and Brazil are in many ways remarkably similar: multiethnic and multiracial, resource-rich, relatively young democracies with a penchant for an exceptionalist view of their histories.

Despite national affinities, U.S.-Brazil relations have often been characterized by misperception and misunderstanding, most recently demonstrated by conflict over how best to contain Iran's nuclear program. This disagreement was instructive to both countries: the United States learned to anticipate independence from Brazil and both countries learned that expressions of friendship do not easily translate into coordinated action. Brazil also learned that engagement in Iran's nuclear program risks diluting its credentials to negotiate on other issues of international concern. But Brazil and the United States have begun a dialogue on cooperation regarding food security and labor rights in the Middle East, following the upheaval in the Arab world. In addition, Brazil and the United States are collaborating on a number of issues in third countries in the Americas and Africa.

The Obama-Rousseff meetings in Brazil earlier this year were a signal that both countries are willing to forge closer ties on bilateral, regional, and global issues. Obama's trip, at a time of heightened tensions in the Middle East and military action in Libya, underscored the U.S. desire to put relations on a more positive track. The Task Force welcomes the ten new bilateral agreements that the two presidents signed, which include accords on biofuels, use of space, educational exchange, promotion of decent work in third countries, and—significantly—a framework to negotiate new commercial and economic agreements.[44] Still, the Task

Force is concerned that no mechanism exists in the U.S. government to coordinate these initiatives and drive policy toward Brazil.

RECENT HISTORY

Aside from a brief period of alignment after the 1964 military coup, Brazil has largely avoided a "special relationship" with the United States. Despite a history of misperception and cautious distancing, most Brazilians—swept up by Obama's 2008 campaign and election—marveled at and delighted in the fact that the United States had elected an African-American man with a message of multilateralism and open-mindedness. Obama's recognition of an evolving U.S. role in the global order led many Brazilians to believe that the U.S. relationship with Latin America, and with Brazil especially, would evolve and improve. Obama's speech at the April 2009 Summit of the Americas about a more equal relationship with the region only reaffirmed this expectation.[45]

Yet the remainder of 2009 dispelled hopes in the region for a sea change in U.S. policy toward Latin America. The U.S. approach to two particular issues—the coup in Honduras and military bases in Colombia—drew the two countries into direct tension. Although these issues have receded for now, they are nonetheless instructive because they reflect the differences in how Brazil and the United States see the world.

The disagreements did not prevent Brazil and the United States from advancing cooperation on discrete issues. In early 2010, Secretary Clinton made a multi-stop trip to Latin America, spending a day in Brazil and signing a number of bilateral agreements.[46] Shortly after Clinton's visit, Brazil and the United States settled an eight-year trade dispute over U.S. subsidies to cotton growers in a resolution that negotiators hailed as innovative.[47]

Just eight months after the Brazilian criticism of the Colombia base deal and even as tensions over Iran grew, U.S. secretary of defense Robert M. Gates and Brazilian defense minister Nelson Jobim signed the U.S.-Brazil Defense Cooperation Agreement (DCA) in April 2010. The DCA is an umbrella agreement that lays the groundwork for further cooperation on issues of defense, intelligence, and security, and is the first arrangement of its kind between the two countries since 1977.

IRAN

Despite growing potential on the bilateral front, forging cooperative ties on an international security issue—Iran—proved much more difficult. Early in Obama's presidency, he and Lula discussed containing Iran's nuclear ambitions. Lula and his foreign minister understood, some say mistakenly, the White House to have offered a green light to pursue what ultimately became the Brazil-Turkey nuclear fuel swap deal negotiated with Iran in spring 2010.[48] Brazil envisioned the deal as the first step toward ensuring that Iran's nuclear program remained peaceful. But by the time the agreement was reached, the United States and other P5 members had grown convinced that sanctions were the best strategy for bringing Iran to the negotiating table. Indeed, Washington asked Brazil to support the sanctions and had dispatched Clinton to Brazil in March 2010 to solicit Brasília's cooperation. After the nuclear fuel swap agreement was announced and after Washington's negative reaction, Brazil manifested its sense of betrayal with a "no" vote at the Security Council on a new round of sanctions.

Though it seems that Rousseff has deemphasized the security dimension of relations with Iran, Brazil's initiative to negotiate with Iran last year was not merely a product of the personalities in office at the time. Rather, engagement with Iran demonstrated Brazil's belief in the intrinsic value of its participation and contribution on major international security issues. Brazil paid a high cost, domestically and diplomatically, for the failure of the initiative in the short term. To date, the Rousseff administration has steered clear of engaging again on this issue. Brazil's participation alerted the major powers to its presence on global security issues and served notice that Brazil would remain a significant international actor.

Conclusions and Recommendations

The Iran experience illustrates the need for the two countries to establish mechanisms to anticipate and mitigate against misunderstandings and conflicting views of international security issues. The Task Force strongly recommends institutionalizing a process of open and regular communication between the countries' two presidents and their respective senior officials. Differing perspectives are bound to arise between two large, complicated countries, but neither country should allow those to color the totality of the relationship.

NUCLEAR SECURITY

As Brazil aspires to become a major exporter of processed uranium, one goal of Brazil's opposition to sanctions against Iran was surely to protect Brazil's burgeoning enrichment industry and the potential global market for nuclear energy.

The Task Force acknowledges the positive role Brazil is playing with respect to nuclear security in South America via the web of bilateral cooperation and inspection of nuclear facilities between Brazil and Argentina. Likewise, the Task Force recognizes Brazil's view that the bilateral inspection regime—and the broader safeguards regime established under the quadripartite Comprehensive Safeguards Agreement between Brazil, Argentina, the Argentine-Brazilian Agency for Accounting and Control (ABACC), and the International Atomic Energy Agency (IAEA)—helps explain Brazil's (and Argentina's) reluctance to sign the IAEA's more invasive Additional Protocol.

Though Washington and Brasília remain at odds over Brazil's reluctance to adopt the Additional Protocol, the Task Force believes that the Additional Protocol plays a fundamental role in promoting global nuclear security and that universal adoption of it is an important goal. Moreover, given Brazil's commitment to nonproliferation and its growing peaceful nuclear energy industry, the Task Force anticipates that Brazil will continue to have an important role in the shaping of international nuclear policy. The Task Force thus recommends that the United States and Brazil pursue bilateral discussions in advance of the 2012 Nuclear Security Summit in Seoul and continue their multilateral discussions through the Nuclear Suppliers Group (NSG) to work toward the strengthening of international standards governing nuclear export controls.

The Task Force recognizes that in the near term, Brazil is unlikely to accept a change in the NSG guidelines that would require adoption of the Additional Protocol as a condition of nuclear technology supply. Over the short term, therefore, the Task Force recommends that the United States propose a bridging solution to Brazil, wherein the terms of ABACC's safeguards framework can voluntarily be made more consistent with the spirit of the Additional Protocol. The United States should, however, maintain its long-term goal of updating NSG guidelines to win universal adoption of the Additional Protocol and requiring it as a condition of nuclear technology supply. In addition, the United

States should maintain the long-term goal of pursuing deep cuts in nuclear weapons arsenals.

U.S.-BRAZIL TRADE AND INVESTMENT

Trade relations between the United States and Brazil have grown dramatically over the past decade, total trade in goods rising from $28.2 billion in 2002 to a peak of $60.7 billion in 2008.[49] As trade has grown, friction points have also become more apparent. Recent examples include the 2010 WTO authorization for Brazil to impose retaliatory tariffs against U.S. cotton subsidies (resolved for the time being) and the ongoing case regarding U.S. antidumping measures against Brazilian orange juice.

The United States is also a leading direct investor in Brazil, total FDI stocks reaching $56.7 billion in 2009, primarily in manufacturing and finance and insurance sectors. Despite the difficulty for some foreign companies to compete fairly with domestic actors in the Brazilian market, the U.S. private sector is increasingly bullish about doing business in Brazil because the country has significantly improved issues of corruption, contract law, negotiations, and compliance with international business norms over the past several decades. However, the U.S. share of FDI in Brazil relative to GDP has declined over the past fifteen years.

Brazilian multinationals have also increasingly invested in the United States, with total FDI stocks reaching $780 million in 2008. Gerdau, a major Brazilian steel manufacturer, bought AmeriSteel in 1999 and used the company as a platform for further North American acquisitions over the past decade. The Belgian-Brazilian brewer ImBev merged with Anheuser-Busch in 2008, creating the fifth-largest consumer goods company in the world, controlling 25 percent of the global brewing market.

Recommendations

The absence of a bilateral tax treaty (BTT) is a major complication for many U.S. companies looking to establish operations in Brazil. A BTT would eliminate double taxation on investment. Brazil is the only country with a GNP greater than $1 trillion that does not have a BTT with the United States. To encourage Brazilians to do business in the United

States and vice versa, the Task Force recommends that both governments take steps to reduce or altogether eliminate double taxation by
working toward a bilateral tax treaty and to pursue reforms toward a
fair climate for foreign investment.

THIRD COUNTRY, SUBNATIONAL, AND PRIVATE-SECTOR COOPERATION

The richest and deepest connections between Brazil and the United
States tend not to involve direct bilateral relations between the governments, but rather third-country or subnational collaboration and
private-sector partnerships. Some of the most promising collabora-
tions between Brazil and the United States take place outside both
countries' borders on counternarcotics, health and development goals,
promotion of decent work, and biofuels cooperation.

The Task Force finds that there is ample room for the federal governments of the United States and Brazil to capitalize on the relationships being built in third countries and by the countries' governors,
private sectors, trade unions, and civil society organizations. The
growth of these secondary and tertiary interactions presents an
opportunity to build confidence and demonstrate commonality to the
two societies, at the same time laying the groundwork for more struc-
tured bilateral relations that benefit from the confidence and partnerships already in place.

COUNTERNARCOTICS

Counternarcotics efforts in Bolivia represent an opportunity for effective third-country cooperation that maximizes Brazilian and U.S. capabilities and allows for all three countries to learn from one another. Just
weeks after Evo Morales expelled the U.S. Drug Enforcement Agency
(DEA) from Bolivia in 2008, Brazil and Bolivia announced a strategic
alliance to combat drug production and trafficking. Brazil has a significant national interest in Bolivia's drug war: the shared Brazilian-
Bolivian border is longer than that between the United States and
Mexico, and Brazil's police estimate that 60 percent of cocaine entering the country comes from Bolivia.[50]

Brazilians have acknowledged that they are unable to match the U.S. capacity to fund Bolivian police forces and equip them with expensive hardware like patrol helicopters. In August 2009, just eight months after the Brazil-Bolivia treaty went into effect, officials from Brazil's Ministry of External Relations—or Itamaraty—began a series of discussions with U.S. diplomats about Bolivia's interest in trilateral cooperation with the United States. According to American diplomats, the Brazilian willingness to collaborate with the United States on counternarcotics signaled "a significant departure" from the status quo and an "about face" within Itamaraty.[51]

Trilateral counternarcotics efforts in Bolivia have the potential for greater effectiveness in reducing coca cultivation and drug trafficking, and increase opportunities for discussion, partnership, and confidence-building between Brazil and the United States. At the same time, while advancing a common agenda, the United States and Brazil can capitalize on their comparative advantages. The United States provides experience and funding but avoids leaving a heavy footprint. Brazil—without the storied and controversial U.S. counternarcotics profile in the region—takes on greater responsibility, living up to expectations that a regional powerhouse uses its resources for the good of the neighborhood. Currently, negotiations are under way with the Bolivian government about joint monitoring efforts. Despite good intentions and a high degree of openness and cooperation between Brazil and the United States, successful trilateral collaboration requires a commitment from Bolivia in addition to the existing goodwill and bilateral consensus.

Conclusions and Recommendations

The Task Force welcomes Brazil's involvement in counternarcotics, harm reduction, and transnational crime issues on its borders, especially in Bolivia, and encourages other such cooperation between Brazil and the United States elsewhere. The Task Force encourages Brazil's leadership as a voice for reform of the region's counternarcotics strategy.

The Task Force supports Brazil's promotion, by former president Cardoso with former presidents Ricardo Lagos (Chile), Ernesto Zedillo (Mexico), and César Gaviria (Colombia), of harm reduction policies (which treat drug use as a public health issue and promote the reduction of drug consumption) in addition to interdiction and eradication.[52] The Task Force encourages the DEA and USAID and their

Brazilian counterparts working in Bolivia to reinforce one another's efforts to reassure the Bolivian government that outside counternarcotics support—like monitoring of coca cultivation and eradication—does not threaten Bolivian sovereignty.

HEALTH AND DEVELOPMENT

Brazil and the United States are working together on development and health issues in Central America and the Caribbean and in lusophone Africa. Indeed, ABC and USAID have now stationed staff in one another's agencies to advance third-country cooperation. For example, Brazilian and U.S. health and aid institutions support the U.S.-Brazil-Mozambique trilateral technical assistance cooperation that works to strengthen the Mozambican response to its HIV/AIDS epidemic. In 2010, a USAID-ABC-Embrapa partnership launched a program to support NGOs that will establish food security projects in Mozambique. In São Tomé and Príncipe, off the West Coast of Africa, Brazil and the United States have committed to multiyear funding for an antimalaria project. In El Salvador, Brazilian and U.S. entities are helping develop a National Public Health Institute.

Even before the 2010 earthquake, U.S. and Brazilian officials had identified Haiti as ground where the two countries could work together. In 2009, ABC and USAID made a joint trip to Port-au-Prince to explore trilateral cooperation opportunities, including joint technical assistance to train garment sector workers and U.S. Southern Command collaboration with the Brazilian engineering battalion of MINUSTAH on infrastructure projects. After the earthquake and under the auspices of the Brazilian-led UN mission, the United States and Brazil have worked together, along with a number of other partners, to provide security and rebuild infrastructure in Haiti.

Conclusions and Recommendations

The Task Force welcomes deepening U.S.-Brazil cooperation on health and development in the Americas and Africa. Brazil's private-sector investment and engagement in Africa, along with U.S.-Brazil efforts toward capacity building (like USAID-ABC joint projects) and in agriculture, biofuels, and public health, has the potential to shift the continent's development paradigm away from the provision of inefficient aid money and the often exploitative Chinese resource drive.

In the Americas, the Task Force likewise encourages USAID and ABC to advance cooperation in Haiti and applauds existing bilateral and multilateral collaboration under Brazil's leadership of MINUS-TAH. Also in the Caribbean, the Task Force considers that the United States can learn from Brazil's presence in Cuba. The Brazilian government and private sector engages Cubans across a number of issues and industries, including energy and agriculture, and can share instructive experience with respect to the many dimensions of Cuba's transition.

Colombia is fruitful ground for U.S.-Brazil collaboration on gender, health, security, and social issues. More than three million Colombians (largely women and children of indigenous or African descent) have been displaced from their land, making them, according to the UN High Commission for Refugees, the world's largest population of internally displaced persons (IDPs). Arguably, a critical dimension of resolving Colombia's conflict resides in a sound rural strategy that includes the redistribution of ill-gotten land, among other measures.[53] To advance peace and security in Colombia, Brazil and the United States each have significant resources and expertise that together could help Colombia protect and assist its IDPs and develop its rural regions in a socially, economically, and environmentally sustainable way.

BIOFUELS

Developing biofuel programs in the Western Hemisphere is a principal goal of a 2007 MOU signed by Brazil and the United States. In 2009, the two countries agreed to expand science cooperation on standards and research on biofuels.

El Salvador and Haiti were among the first nations, along with the Dominican Republic and St. Kitts and Nevis, to receive bilateral biofuels assistance from Brazil and the United States. In 2008, Brazil and the United States expanded this biofuel cooperation to include Guatemala, Honduras, Jamaica, Guinea-Bissau, and Senegal. These primarily Central American and Caribbean countries benefit from the development of biofuels for domestic consumption. At the same time, expanding these markets aims to entice investors into producing biofuels in the region, which has preferential access to the U.S. market through the Caribbean Basin Initiative. (The Task Force encourages lifting U.S. protectionist measures that limit the expansion of Brazilian biofuels in the American market, as discussed earlier.) Brazil is also in the early stages of helping Cuba develop its nascent biofuels capacity.

Recommendations

The Task Force encourages the expansion of the existing U.S.-Brazil biofuels program to include a greater number of developing countries, and also to include demand-side support, such as the diffusion of flex-fuel vehicles.

CLIMATE CHANGE

U.S.-Brazil subnational cooperation to combat climate change does not necessarily contradict bilateral national climate change efforts, though these state-to-state and regional agreements reflect a sense on the ground that the high-level agreements are neither adequately ambitious nor meeting their goals.

Initiatives such as the California Global Warming Solutions Act of 2006 (AB32 set the 2020 greenhouse gas emissions reduction goal into law), and the Regional Greenhouse Gas Initiative (a market-based regulatory program to reduce greenhouse gas emissions), which comprised ten northeastern and mid-Atlantic states in the United States, both go well beyond current U.S. federal standards in limiting greenhouse gas emissions. With the UN Framework Convention on Climate Change process unfolding slowly, then California governor Arnold Schwarzenegger inaugurated the first Governors' Global Climate Change Summit in 2008, which initiated subnational climate change collaboration programs in which Brazilian states played a significant role.

Conclusions and Recommendations

Bilateral climate initiatives on the state and regional level can enhance climate cooperation between the United States and Brazil. The Task Force recommends relevant executive branch and congressional offices endeavor to understand and anticipate the significant foreign policy consequences of subnational projects.

PRIVATE SECTOR

The Task Force finds that connectivity between the United States and Brazil is often driven not by their governments, but by the private sector. Even when the public-sector agenda between these countries has seemed thin, business-to-business ties have grown at a robust pace, bringing the two countries closer together than ever before. Indeed, the U.S. and Brazilian private sectors tend to understand each other better than government officials. Though the two governments help convene the semiannual meetings of the U.S.-Brazil CEO forum (a group of ten Brazilian and ten American CEOs from a range of industries), and senior government officials address the group, the impetus for the six-year-old endeavor derives from the business communities in each country, which recognize opportunities in one another but confront a number of barriers that limit trade, investment, and commerce.

The forum has made progress on visa reform (extending visa validity in Brazil from five to ten years) and aviation liberalization (increasing passenger flights by 50 percent since 2008), and has taken steps to encourage a BTT. However, the current visa requirements for travelers remain burdensome. The Brazilian-American Chamber of Commerce and the Brazil-U.S. Business Council are two examples of private-sector institutions working to develop closer trade and investment ties between the two countries.

Recommendations

To increase and facilitate commerce between Brazil and the United States, as well as to boost social and cultural connectivity, the Task Force recommends that the United States take the first step to waive visa requirements for Brazilians by immediately reviewing Brazil's criteria for participation in the Visa Waiver Program. Such a move will undoubtedly be reciprocated by Brazil for American travelers.

To make this significant step viable, the Task Force recommends robust bilateral consultations between the U.S. Department of Homeland Security and its counterpart organizations in Brazil. Given the increasing flow and connectivity between private sectors, the Task Force recommends a social security portability agreement, which would provide benefits to citizens of both countries, including the avoidance of double taxation on benefits.

Conclusion

President Obama's visit to Brazil in March 2011 heralded a new phase of the U.S.-Brazil relationship. With agreements that touched on a wide range of issues—including trade and finance, infrastructure investment, civil aviation, energy, labor, education, and social concerns—presidents Obama and Rousseff signaled to their respective countries that this bilateral relationship is poised to evolve into a robust and mature friendship among equals. Yet most of the concrete deliverables announced during the trip reflected only the low-hanging fruit of cooperation.

If the United States and Brazil are invested in a serious and deepening relationship, their conversation must continue. As in U.S. relations with such powers as India, China, Russia, or Germany, frank and high-level dialogue with Brazil will allow both countries to identify, acknowledge, and manage issues of potential disagreement, which should not destabilize the relationship in its entirety.

Along these lines, the Task Force recommends that Obama host an interministerial meeting with Brazil, as President George W. Bush did in 2003. Principals from the U.S. and Brazilian governments need to communicate openly and specifically about the issues that remain as obstacles, including: trade, market access, and subsidies; priorities for and approaches to international security abroad; UN Security Council reform; and exercising human rights values. With frameworks now established for dialogue on many of these issues, the two countries can make genuine progress.

COMMON GROUND

Similar domestic challenges should serve as common ground between Brazil and the United States. Rousseff's domestic priorities—quality education for all, innovation in science and technology, access to quality public health care, and infrastructure projects (PAC and PAC II)—should resonate strongly with Obama and his administration as the United States itself works to improve in each of these. With an understanding that the political environments surrounding each administration are markedly different, the two governments can share best practices and further develop dialogues among the experts who work on these domestic initiatives.

The United States should expect the Brazilian expression of shared values—free markets, rule of law, individual rights, religious freedom, and diversity and equality—to look quite different from its own. Yet shared values and many common goals mean that each country has a stake in the other's success. The Task Force expects that Brazil will continue to define its national interest independently from the United States, and the United States cannot decide where and how Brazil will engage internationally. Still, many of the Task Force's recommendations are designed to create an environment in which Brazilian foreign policy decisions might well reinforce U.S. foreign policy goals.

MATURE PARTNERSHIP

The Task Force does not expect nor does it recommend that Brazil and the United States pursue any special relationship. Instead, the Task Force encourages U.S. policymakers to recognize that Brazil and the United States can have a mature working relationship on bilateral and global issues without complete alignment across the board. Obama set a good example in this regard: standing alongside Rousseff in Brasília, he hailed Brazil's leadership on peace, security, and other global issues, just one day after Brazil (along with China, Russia, India, and Germany) abstained on the UNSC vote to authorize a no-fly zone in Libya.

Treating each other as equals is fundamentally a matter of diplomacy and respect: it does not imply that the United States and Brazil operate within the same global context. The United States will continue to exercise its influence on a different scale and with different instruments than Brazil. At the same time, Brazil will continue to engage—economically and diplomatically—in regions and on issues well beyond South America. As these two countries increasingly intersect on the defining international issues of the day, the U.S. government must begin to incorporate the prospect for cooperation with Brazil into its global strategic vision.

POLICY COORDINATION

In both Brazil and the United States, interagency coordination of over-all policy toward one another is limited. This is especially true in the United States, where initiatives regarding Brazil are undertaken by a variety of agencies with little or no synchronization or guiding strategy.[54] The Task Force believes that existing joint efforts and potential areas for cooperation would benefit from each country developing a more cohesive and coordinated approach toward the other.

Brazil's growing geostrategic importance merits sustained, senior-level, and comprehensive coordination of U.S. policy across agencies. The Task Force cautions that incorporating Brazil into high-level U.S. policy discussions—whether over peace and security, global finance, or climate change—are not likely to succeed if left to the regional director-ates or bureaus at various executive branch agencies or to the regional subcommittees in the Congress.

As Brazil expands its reach across the globe and solidifies its involve-ment on a wide array of international issues, the Task Force recom-mends that the National Security Council institutionalize a standing interagency coordination mechanism so that a range of U.S. agencies responsible for functional issues such as finance, trade, energy, envi-ronment, agriculture, health, homeland security, defense, and diplo-macy better coordinate what remains a highly decentralized U.S. policy toward Brazil. This would require an NSC director for Brazil, rather than a director for Brazil and the Southern Cone.

The goal is to give Brazil more and better coordinated attention across the U.S. government and to have agencies and departments beyond those that work on Western Hemisphere issues participate in formulating a more comprehensive policy. Within the State Depart-ment, the Task Force recommends creating an Office for Brazilian Affairs separate from the Southern Cone office of the Western Hemi-sphere Affairs bureau.

SEIZING THE MOMENTUM

Cooperation between the United States and Brazil holds too much promise for miscommunication or inevitable disagreements to stand in the way of potential gains. A strengthened U.S.-Brazil relationship could be the basis for economic growth in Brazil, the United States, and globally, as well as for lasting peace and democratic stability in the region, nuclear nonproliferation, international progress on combating climate change, development of a global renewable energy market, global food security, and more legitimate and effective international institutions. Presidents Obama and Rousseff have laid the groundwork for progress on many of these fronts. The moment to build on this positive foundation is now.

Additional Views

In the tradition of Task Force reports, we hold individual views on a number of the subjects addressed, but we strongly concur with the report's core message that U.S. policymakers should recognize "Brazil's standing as a global actor, treat its emergence as an opportunity for the United States, and work with Brazil to develop complementary policies."

Our additional view relates to the recommendation that "the Obama administration now fully endorse Brazil's permanent UNSC membership." We agree with the merits of the case for Brazil's inclusion as a permanent member. We believe that a more gradual approach would likely have more success in navigating the diplomatic complexities presented by U.S. support for Brazil.

There is realistically only room for one permanent member from Latin America—in Asia, by contrast, the consensus view is that there could be two new members—and this presents a difficult issue of priorities for the United States in its own region. This does not mean that Brazil is not the right choice. Rather, considerable diplomatic groundwork should be laid first to deal with the adverse reactions of key U.S. allies who would view the choice of Brazil as directly blocking their own multilateral ambitions. Moreover, the U.S. Congress must be consulted and persuaded to ensure adequate support for a policy change of this importance. Failure to lay all this groundwork first could jeopardize the ultimate success of U.S. support for Brazil's quest for permanent membership.

Thus, we support the position of the United States as articulated by President Obama in Brazil in March 2011, although we agree with the Task Force report's sense of urgency. Accordingly, we would urge the Obama administration to immediately begin to lay the groundwork to permit the United States to endorse Brazil's permanent UNSC membership, rather than the report's recommendation to start with the endorsement and engage later in the groundwork.

Louis E. Caldera, Nelson W. Cunningham, Eli Whitney Debevoise II, Paula J. Dobriansky, José A. Fourquet, Sergio J. Galvis, Kevin P. Green, Brian D. O'Neill, Riordan Roett

This report makes an important contribution to the evolution of American foreign policy thinking about Brazil. In particular, that the report recognizes Brazil's emerging role as a global power and no longer views Brazil primarily through the limiting and distortionary lens of hemispheric affairs are significant, if long overdue, contributions.

That said, the report should, we believe, have gone further. It appropriately recommends the United States immediately support Brazil's candidacy for the United Nations Security Council. However, the report offers additional recommendations for hemispheric consultations and intensive negotiations with Brazil on the matter that create conditions quite different from those under which the United States supported India's candidacy for such a role. We feel this sends the wrong message to Brazil and to the world. If the United States supports, as the Obama administration has said it does, leadership structures in international institutions that are more reflective of international realities, it must support without qualifications Brazil's candidacy. As the world's fifth most populous country, its eighth-largest economy and its likely near-term ascendancy to being the fifth-largest economy, it would be counterproductive for Brazil not to be included among the top tier of major powers whether within the Security Council or other international forums.

The report also carries a suggestion that Brazil not be involved in security affairs in the Middle East. We feel it would be inappropriate for either a report such as this or for the United States to seek to dictate how Brazil pursues its national interests around the world. While differences may occur as a result, one of the most important conclusions of this report is recognizing that differences are to be expected in relationships such as those we are developing with rising major powers such as Brazil, India, and China. Given that America's most important challenge in the multipolar era ahead will be forging new coalitions in which emerging players—like Brazil—can and must play an important role, the United States will need to work to move beyond old attitudes and treat these countries with the respect they have long deserved.

Shepard L. Forman, Donna J. Hrinak, David J. Rothkopf, Julia E. Sweig, Tanisha N. Tingle-Smith

Since this report was completed there have been disturbing developments on the human rights front as the Brazilian government recently announced its official approval for the construction of the $17 billion Belo Monte Dam, which indigenous groups, the human rights community, and environmental activists have opposed for decades. Earlier this year, the Inter-American Commission on Human Rights (IACHR) had stipulated that the Brazilians suspend all facets of the project until certain criteria were met. In addition to ignoring those demands, President Rousseff has broken relations with the IACHR in response, recalling Brazil's ambassador to the Organization of America States and announcing plans to withhold their annual contribution to the IACHR. Not only is it unsettling that the government is moving forward with the dam, but in the process it is damaging the Inter-American human rights system and the commission, which is one of the most effective Inter-American bodies that exists. The Brazilian government needs to reengage with the commission in resolving this seeming impasse.

Joy Olson

Endnotes

1. The Council on Foreign Relations last undertook a Task Force on Brazil in 2001. CFR's February 2001 Independent Task Force report, *A Letter to the President and a Memorandum on Brazil*, is available online at http://www.cfr.org/brazil/letter-president-memorandum-us-policy-toward-brazil/p3900.
2. For the purposes of this report, biofuels refers specifically to alcohol-based fuels.
3. Bolsa Familia, a social welfare program initiated by former president Lula, provides cash transfers to families conditional on primary school attendance and basic medical care for children.
4. Sales of raw materials account for approximately 43 percent of Brazilian exports, up from 23 percent just ten years ago. Vincent Bevins, "Is Brazil too dependent on exporting basic goods?" FinancialTimes.com, July 12, 2010, http://blogs.ft.com/beyond-brics/2010/07/12/is-brazil-too-dependent-on-exporting-basic-goods/ (accessed October 4, 2010).
5. However, a supply shortfall coupled with rampant domestic demand led Brazil to temporarily import ethanol from the United States in early 2011.
6. The promise and challenges of Brazil's energy sector are so fundamental to the contours of the new Brazil that energy is addressed in greater depth in the final section of this report.
7. Strands of soya and wheat, historically grown in temperate climates like South Dakota and Korea, have been altered to grow in tropical Brazil. An army of thousands of trucks spread tens of millions of tons of lime across soils in the central farming belt of the country throughout the late 1990s and early 2000s. The lime reduced acidity in the soil to levels at which crops can grow, effectively creating new farmland on what had been dusty rolling hills.
8. *Clase C* is Brazil's middle class, which earns between R$1,115 and R$4,807 per month and is bracketed by classes A and B and classes D and E.
9. However, with median monthly incomes between R$2,950 and R$5,350, the wealthier *clase B* spent approximately R$1 trillion in 2010 and may still be the primary driver of Brazil's consumer economy.
10. Education shortcomings result in part from high levels of grade repetition, inefficient disbursement of funding by states and municipalities, and too little local government spending on development programs not related to education, which have been shown to matter at least as much for education outcomes as spending on education per se.
11. Brazilian firms require a median of nearly six weeks to fill a skilled vacancy, compared with four weeks in South Africa and just two weeks in India and China.
12. China, by comparison, devotes 1.54 percent of GDP to R&D, which amounts to 5.27 times Brazilian gross spending on investment. Russia spends 1.04 percent of its GDP on R&D, slightly more than Brazil in gross terms. The U.S. share of 2.77 percent nets it 17.30 times gross Brazilian spending.

13. Commodities exports are directly dependent on market pricing and foreign demand and are thereby most vulnerable to external shock.

14. Christophe de Gouvello, "Brazil Low-carbon Country Case Study," World Bank Group, May 31, 2010, p. xxvii.

15. Brazil emits an average of 1.4 metric tons of carbon dioxide (t CO_2) per ton of oil equivalent (toe) energy consumed—less than 60 percent of the global average of 2.41 t CO_2 per toe.

16. The Cerrado is Brazil's savannah region.

17. "Fact Sheet: U.S.-Brazil Strategic Energy Dialogue," http://www.whitehouse.gov/sites/default/files/uploads/Brazil_Strategic_Energy_Partnership.pdf.

18. According the U.S. Energy Information Administration, proven reserves are estimated quantities that analysis of geologic and engineering data demonstrates with reasonable certainty are recoverable under existing economic and operating conditions.

19. Brazil is already a net oil exporter, but imports lighter grades of oil, diesel, and naphtha to fill gaps in domestic production.

20. These estimates are lower than Petrobras's official projections.

21. Biomass provides a further 5 percent of generation; nuclear power, natural gas, and coal-fired plants account for the rest.

22. The Intergovernmental Panel on Climate Change reports that the majority of global climate models indicate an increase in precipitation in southern Brazil and a decrease in northeastern Brazil under a wide range of future scenarios. Projections for the Amazon basin are less reliable, however, with wide disagreement among models even under similar scenarios.

23. Flex-fuel vehicles reached 94 percent of Brazil's new car sales in August 2009, and by March 2010 Brazil had more than ten million flex-fuel vehicles on the road.

24. The monitoring systems are coordinated by the National Institute for Space Research (INPE) and the Brazilian Institute of the Environment and Natural Resources (Ibama).

25. Related financing mechanisms include the Green Protocol, requiring state banks to ensure the sustainability of projects they finance, environmentally oriented taxes and credit restrictions on rural environmental offenders, and major funds, such as the National Fund on Climate Change and the Amazon Fund. These two funds in particular have broad mandates to combat climate change on a system-wide level, integrating specific reduction projects with efforts to improve research, education, communication, and policymaking.

26. Though commonly used, the business-as-usual baseline is not a particularly well-defined measure, varies by country, and can be subject to industry interests.

27. Some 79 percent of the Cerrado has already been converted to agricultural use. While conversion of the Cerrado forest emits less carbon dioxide than conversion of the Amazon, preservation of the Cerrado is important because it maintains a high level of biodiversity.

28. The CDM allows Annex I countries (those with binding emissions reduction targets) to fund emissions-reduction projects in non–Annex I countries (which do not have binding targets) and use the resulting credits to partially meet their own reduction goals.

29. More than 70 percent of registered projects are sponsored by EU countries that can use the resulting credits within the EU carbon trading system.

30. Developing countries are often referred to as part of the Global South, a categorization that evolved from Cold War–era delineations between the First, Second, and Third Worlds.

31. As a founding member of the League of Nations, Brazil tried and failed in 1919 to obtain a permanent seat on the body's Council for the Principal Allied and Associated

Powers. Brazil has been elected a nonpermanent member of the UNSC five times in the post–Cold War era and a record ten times overall. In line with wider efforts to expand the influence of nontraditional powers, Brazil has worked with other non-P5 countries to pursue a permanent seat on a remodeled Security Council.

32. Barack Obama, "Remarks by President Obama and President Rousseff of Brazil in Brasília, Brazil," March 19, 2011, Palacio do Planalto.

33. Lally Weymouth, "What Does It Mean to You To Be the First Female President of Brazil?" *Washington Post,* December 3, 2010, http://www.washingtonpost.com/wp-dyn/content/article/2010/12/03/AR2010120303241.html.

34. See http://www.whitehouse.gov/sites/default/files/uploads/Brazil_ATEC.pdf.

35. The G20 took on increasing importance during the global financial crisis of 2008 and 2009 and was elevated to head-of-state-level meetings. During the 2009 summit in Pittsburgh, the G20 officially replaced the G8 as the premier forum for global economic coordination.

36. Since 2008, developing and transition countries have gained 4.59 points in voting power within the World Bank, increasing their total voting power to 47.19 percent. Brazil's share has risen from 2.07 to 2.24 percent. In the IMF, Brazil now has 1.38 percent of voting rights. In October 2010, in advance of the G20 summit in South Korea, G20 finance ministers agreed to reallocate more than 6 percent of IMF voting rights to emerging economies and to reassign two board seats previously held by Europeans. The IMF managing director has called the agreement, approved in December 2010, "historical" and "the biggest reform ever in the governance of the institution." The reforms, supported by the United States, place Brazil within the fund's ten largest shareholders.

37. "Ignore Brazil's Election, Here Are the Real Problems Facing the Country," *Stratfor,* October 5, 2010.

38. Chile, however, tops Colombia in total trade flows with Brazil.

39. Paulo Vieira da Cunha, "The Brazilian Economy—The Choices for Dilma," lecture, Inter-American Dialogue, Washington, DC, November 10, 2010.

40. Associate members of Mercosul are Bolivia, Chile, Colombia, Ecuador, and Peru.

41. The Central Bank reports that as many as eight hundred Brazilian firms invest abroad; Central and South America receive the greatest share of Brazilian investment at 23.2 percent. In turn, these regions are responsible for 32.3 percent of the foreign revenues of Brazilian firms investing abroad. BNDES has extended loans or lines of credit to Brazilian companies in Argentina, Chile, Costa Rica, Cuba, the Dominican Republic, Ecuador, El Salvador, Honduras, Mexico, Paraguay, Peru, Uruguay, and Venezuela. In Argentina, for example, approximately 30 percent of foreign investment comes from Brazil.

42. Though Latin Americans tend to deride Brazil for its economic self-interest, Brazil points instead to examples where it has put stability and regional development above individual national interest. In 2007, for example, Brazil agreed to reduce Paraguayan debt owed as a result of the 1973 Treaty of Itaipú, which specified that Brazil essentially finance the entire construction of the shared hydroelectric Itaipú dam, and that resource-strapped Paraguay would repay Brazil through amortized payments deducted from the electric energy that it sold exclusively to Brazil. Paraguayans widely view Itaipú as a symbol of Brazilian dominance. Indeed, the Paraguayan deputy foreign minister asserted that the original fifty-year deal reflected "the realpolitik of an ant staring up at an elephant." In 2009, Lula renegotiated the terms of the treaty, promising to triple compensation paid to Paraguay for its unused electricity and pledging the construction of a transmission line to Asunción. For some in Brazil, Lula's gesture was viewed as a concession with an air of altruism. For Paraguay and others in Latin America, the move was a step to correct the historically unjust arrangement.

43. For example, see Lisa Kubiske, "Peres and Abbas Visits in Perspective," U.S. Embassy in Brasília, December 2, 2009.
44. Refer to online appendix of signed bilateral agreements at http://www.cfr.org/ brazil_task_force/.
45. Barack Obama, "Remarks by the President at the Summit of the Americas Opening Ceremony," Port of Spain, Trinidad and Tobago, April 17, 2009.
46. See online appendix of signed bilateral agreements at http://www.cfr.org/brazil_ task_force/.
47. The United States agreed to modify an export loan program and establish a temporary assistance fund for the Brazilian cotton industry. In exchange, Brazil abandoned plans to impose more than $800 million of sanctions, which had been approved by the WTO in 2009.
48. Letter from President Barack Obama to President Luiz Inácio da Silva, April 20, 2010, http://www.politicaexterna.com/11023/brazil-iran-turkey-nuclear-negotiations -obamas-letter-to-lula.
49. Trade declined by 26 percent in 2009, driven largely by a 34 percent decline in U.S. imports from Brazil, but rebounded by 28 percent in 2010 to reach $59.3 billion, supported by a 35 percent surge in U.S. exports. In 2010, the United States exported $35.3 billion worth of goods to Brazil, primarily chemicals, computer and electrical equipment, transportation equipment, and other machinery and fabricated metals. U.S. imports from Brazil were just $23.9 billion, crude oil imports accounting for nearly 33 percent of the total, followed by primary metal manufacturing, agricultural products, and machinery. U.S.-Brazil trade has been largely balanced for the past quarter century; the United States was a net importer from Brazil from 1985 to 1994 before flipping to a net exporter from 1995 to 2001, back to a net importer from 2002 to 2007, and once again a net exporter from 2008 to the present.
50. Carlos Valdez, "Cocaine Flows Over Brazil-Bolivia Border," *Washington Post*, June 10, 2007, http://www.washingtonpost.com/wp-dyn/content/article/2007/06/10/ AR2007061000668_pf.html.
51. Lisa Kubiske, "Keeping I it Brazil and Bolivia's Flickering Interest in Trilateral Counternarcotics Cooperation with the U.S.," U.S. Embassy in Brasília, September 14, 2009.
52. "Drugs and Democracy: Toward a Paradigm Shift," Latin American Commission on Drugs and Democracy, February 11, 2009, http://www.drogasedemocracia.org/Ar- quivos/declaracao_ingles_site.pdf.
53. For more detail, please see the CFR-sponsored Report of an Independent Commission, *Andes 2020: A New Strategy for the Challenges of Colombia and the Region*, http:// www.cfr.org/chile/andes-2020/p6640.
54. Itamaraty—under the current foreign minister—is now developing a department that will streamline U.S.-related policy.

Task Force Members

Jed N. Bailey is an expert in energy markets in developing countries and the founder of the Popo Agie Group, an incubator focused on products and services that promote learning at all ages. He was previously vice president for applied research consulting at IHS CERA, where he was responsible for IHS CERA's global bespoke research and consulting practice. Bailey is the author of over seventy IHS CERA reports and directed IHS CERA multiclient studies that examined the energy futures of Brazil, China, Mexico, South America, and Southeast Asia. He has been widely quoted in publications ranging from the *Economist* and the *Financial Times* to the *Iran Daily* and has appeared on Bloomberg Television and CNN International. His current projects at the Popo Agie Group include developing Kaleidoshapes, a large-scale construction and dramatic play toy for young children; experimenting with the graphical presentation of complex data; and exploring the use of narrative in corporate strategy and communications. Bailey holds a BS from the University of Wyoming and an MS from the Massachusetts Institute of Technology.

Samuel W. Bodman served as U.S. secretary of energy from 2005 to 2009 and previously served as deputy secretary of the treasury and as deputy secretary of commerce. Bodman currently serves on the board of directors of the Hess Corporation, the AES Corporation, and Weatherford International. He is a trustee of the Massachusetts Institute of Technology (MIT), Cornell University, and the Carnegie Institution, as well as a lifetime trustee of the Isabella Stewart Gardner Museum. He is a member of the National Academy of Engineering and the American Academy of Arts and Sciences. He is also a chairman of the advisory board of the University of Texas Energy Institute and a member of the energy task force of the Hoover Institution at Stanford University. He serves on the international advisory council of the

King Abdullah University of Science and Technology. Bodman earned a BS from Cornell University and a PhD from MIT, where he was also associate professor of chemical engineering. He began his work in the financial sector as technical director of the American Research and Development Corporation. In 1983 he became president and CEO of Fidelity Investments and a director of the Fidelity Group of Mutual Funds. In 1987, he joined Cabot Corporation, where he served as chairman, CEO, and director.

R. Nicholas Burns is professor of the practice of diplomacy and international politics at the Harvard Kennedy School and director of the future of diplomacy project and faculty chair for the programs on the Middle East and on India and South Asia. He serves on the board of directors of the school's Belfer Center for Science and International Affairs and on the boards of several nonprofit organizations. Ambassador Burns served in the U.S. Foreign Service for twenty-seven years until his retirement in April 2008, serving variously as undersecretary of state for political affairs, U.S. ambassador to NATO and Greece, and State Department spokesman. He was senior director for Russia, Ukraine, and Eurasia affairs on the National Security Council and special assistant to President William J. Clinton and, before that, director for Soviet affairs in the George H.W. Bush administation. He also served at the U.S. consulate in Jerusalem and the U.S. embassies in Egypt and Mauritania. He has received the Secretary of State's Distinguished Service Award, Johns Hopkins University's Woodrow Wilson Award for Public Service, and Boston College's Alumni Achievement Award. He has a BA from Boston College and an MA from the Johns Hopkins School of Advanced International Studies.

Louis E. Caldera is the vice president of programs with the Jack Kent Cooke Foundation, where he leads the foundation's scholarship and grant programs and is responsible for the foundation's communications, information systems, program development, and evaluation functions. Caldera has a distinguished public service career that includes service as an officer in the U.S. Army, as a California legislator, as secretary of the army in the Clinton administration, and as president of the University of New Mexico. He also served in the Clinton administration as managing director and chief operating officer of the Corporation for National and Community Service. Prior to joining the Jack Kent Cooke

Foundation, Caldera was a senior fellow at the Center for American Progress, a progressive think tank, where he focused on higher education, immigration, and other public policy matters affecting poor and ethnically and racially diverse communities in the United States. He served on President Barack Obama's Department of Defense transition team and was an assistant to the president and director of the White House Military Office in the early months of the Obama administration. Caldera is a graduate of the U.S. Military Academy at West Point and holds law and business degrees from Harvard University.

Eileen B. Claussen is the president of the Pew Center on Global Climate Change and Strategies for the Global Environment. Claussen is the former assistant secretary of state for oceans and international environmental and scientific affairs. Prior to joining the Department of State, Claussen served for three years as a special assistant to the president and senior director for global environmental affairs on the National Security Council. She has also served as chairman of the United Nations Multilateral Montreal Protocol Fund. Claussen was director of atmospheric programs at the U.S. Environmental Protection Agency (EPA), where she was responsible for activities related to the depletion of the ozone layer, Title IV of the Clean Air Act, and the EPA's energy efficiency programs. Claussen is a member of the Council on Foreign Relations, the Ecomagination advisory board, the Harvard environmental economics program advisory panel, and the U.S. Commodity Future Trading Commission's advisory committee. She is the recipient of the Department of State's Career Achievement Award and the Distinguished Executive Award for Sustained Extraordinary Accomplishment. She also served as the Timothy Atkeson scholar in residence at Yale University.

Nelson W. Cunningham is managing partner and a cofounder of McLarty Associates. Under his leadership, McLarty Associates has developed into a firm with global reach and over four dozen employees and advisers stationed in Washington and around the world. Cunningham served as special adviser to President Clinton on Western Hemisphere affairs and as general counsel at the White House Office of Administration. He previously served as general counsel to Chairman Joseph R. Biden of the Senate Judiciary Committee, focusing on constitutional, judicial, and criminal justice matters. He also served as an assistant U.S. attorney in the southern district of New York from 1988 to 1994. Cunningham was a campaign adviser and member of the Obama-Biden transition team and was a foreign policy and trade adviser to John Kerry's 2004 presidential campaign as well as to those of other Democratic candidates. He is an active member of the boards of the Institute of the Americas, the Business Council for International Understanding, the American Security Project, and the U.S.-India Business Council and is a member of the Yale president's council on international activities, the Department of State's advisory committee on international economic policy, the Export-Import Bank advisory committee, the Council of the Americas, and the Council on Foreign Relations. Cunningham is a graduate of Yale College and Stanford Law School.

Eli Whitney Debevoise II is a senior partner in the law firm of Arnold & Porter LLP, with particular involvement in international financial transactions, public policy, international arbitration, multijurisdictional litigation, banking, and international trade. The firm acts as legal counsel to Brazil on certain transactional and litigation matters. He rejoined Arnold & Porter LLP in 2010 after serving as U.S. executive director of the World Bank beginning in 2007. During his tenure at the bank, he had a leading role in capital increase and share realignment negotiations and participated in preparations for G8 and G20 summits. Debevoise has lectured at Harvard Law School, Yale Law School, the Tuck School of Business at Dartmouth, and the Hungarian Institute for the Training of Bankers. In 2010, he gave the Lauder leadership lecture at the Lauder Institute at the University of Pennsylvania. He has written articles on sovereign finance, international banking, international arbitration, securities regulation, World Trade Organization dispute resolution, U.S. export controls, and sovereign immunity. Debevoise graduated from Yale University and Harvard Law School. He holds an honorary doctorate in law from the Vermont Law School and is a recipient of the Order of Rio Branco.

Paula J. Dobriansky is the senior vice president and global head of government and regulatory affairs at Thomson Reuters. She is an adjunct senior fellow at Harvard University's John F. Kennedy Belfer Center for Science and International Affairs and holds the distinguished national security chair at the U.S. Naval Academy. From May 2001 to January 2009, Ambassador Dobriansky served as undersecretary of state for democracy and global affairs; in February 2007, she was appointed the president's special envoy on Northern Ireland. She served as senior vice president and director of the Washington office of the Council on Foreign Relations (CFR) and as CFR's first George F. Kennan senior fellow for Russian and Eurasian studies. Her other government appointments include associate director for policy and programs at the United States Information Agency, deputy assistant secretary of state for human rights and humanitarian affairs, and director of European and Soviet affairs on the National Security Council. From 1997 to 2001, she served on the U.S. Advisory Commission on Public Diplomacy. Ambassador Dobriansky received a BSFS from Georgetown University's School of Foreign Service and an MA and PhD from Harvard University. She is a recipient of various honors, including the secretary of state's highest honor, the Distinguished Service Medal.

Shepard L. Forman is director emeritus and senior fellow of the Center on International Cooperation at New York University. Prior to founding the center, he directed the human rights and governance and international affairs programs at the Ford Foundation. He serves on the boards of the International Peace Institute, the Global Fairness Initiative, Peace Dividend Trust, and Scholars at Risk, among others. Forman received his PhD in anthropology from Columbia University and did postdoctoral studies in economic development at the Institute of Development Studies in Sussex, England. He served on the faculty at Indiana University, the University of Chicago, and the University of Michigan and conducted field research in Brazil and East Timor. He has authored two books on Brazil and numerous articles and policy papers on humanitarian assistance and postconflict reconstruction assistance and statebuilding. He is coeditor, with Stewart Patrick, of *Good Intentions: Pledges of Aid to Countries Emerging from Conflict* and *Multilateralism and U.S. Foreign Policy: Ambivalent Engagement*; with Romita Ghosh of *Promoting Reproductive Health: Investing in Health for Development*; and, with Bruce Jones and Richard Gowen, of *Cooperating for Peace and Security*. He also edited *Diagnosing America: Anthropology and Public Policy*, which examines the application of anthropological studies to social problems in the United States.

José A. Fourquet serves as a managing director of the DBS Financial Group, one of the largest financial advisory firms in the state of Florida.

Prior to that, Fourquet worked for four years as a managing director and head of the Miami private investment management branch of Lehman Brothers, Inc. Before joining Lehman, President George W. Bush nominated Fourquet and the U.S. Senate unanimously confirmed him to serve as U.S. executive director of the Inter-American Development Bank from 2001 to 2004. Prior, Fourquet worked for five years as a vice president in the fixed income, currency, and commodities division of Goldman, Sachs & Co., in New York. Fourquet began his career as an operations officer in the Central Intelligence Agency and spent over six years posted abroad in Latin America and the Caribbean, where he collected, evaluated, and reported high-priority intelligence of interest to U.S. policymakers. Fourquet graduated from Georgetown University with a BA in government and a School of Foreign Service special certificate in Latin American studies. He also obtained an MBA in finance from Columbia Business School, where he was inducted into the Beta Gamma Sigma honor society.

Maria C. Freire is president of the Albert and Mary Lasker Foundation. Prior to this, she led the Global Alliance for TB Drug Development, transforming the organization into a world leader in tuberculosis drug development. An internationally recognized expert in technology commercialization, Freire directed the Office of Technology Transfer at the U.S. National Institutes of Health (NIH) and established the Office of Technology Development at the University of Maryland at Baltimore and in Baltimore County. Freire obtained her BS at Universidad Peruana Cayetano Heredia (Lima, Peru) and her PhD in biophysics from the University of Virginia. Active on the NIH advisory committee to the director, the international advisory steering committee of the Instituto Carlos Slim de la Salud (Mexico), the Association of American Medical Colleges advisory panel on research, and the international advisory panel to the Ministerial Working Group on Scaling up of Primary Health Systems, Freire was one of ten commissioners selected for the World Health Organization's Commission on Intellectual Property Rights, Innovation and Public Health (CIPIH). A member of the Institute of Medicine of the National Academies of Science, she has received the Department of Health and Human Services Secretary's Award for Distinguished Service, the Arthur S. Flemming Award, and the Bayh-Dole Award.

Stanley A. Gacek* is a labor lawyer with both U.S. and international experience. He is a recognized expert on Brazilian labor and social issues and is the author of a thorough comparative analysis of the Brazilian and U.S. labor law systems, *Sistemas de Relacoes do Trabalho: Exame dos Modelos Brasil-Estados Unidos.* Gacek is currently serving as international relations officer in the U.S. Department of Labor's Bureau of International Affairs and is responsible for policy and comparative labor law analysis and for representing the U.S. government in its bilateral discussions with counterpart labor ministries throughout the world. Prior to his current job with the Labor Department, Gacek served as special counsel for international labor law at the Solidarity Center/AFL-CIO and associate director of the AFL-CIO's international department. He was the AFL-CIO's international affairs assistant director (Americas Region) from 1997 to 2005. He served as the assistant director for international affairs at the United Food and Commercial Workers International Union (UFCW) from 1984 to 1997 and was the UFCW's assistant general counsel from 1979 to 1984. Gacek received his BA in social studies from Harvard University and his JD from Harvard Law School. He was an adjunct professor at Harvard University in 2008 and has been an active member of the District of Columbia Bar Association.

Sergio J. Galvis is a partner at Sullivan & Cromwell LLP and heads the firm's practice in Brazil and elsewhere in Latin America. For more than twenty-five years, Galvis has worked on hundreds of matters involving parties from more than twenty-five countries in Asia, Europe, and Latin America. His recent experience in Brazil includes the proposed combination of LAN Airlines and TAM S.A. In 2010, he received the Distinguished Global Citizen Award at the Global Kids annual benefit. He was named by the *National Law Journal* as one of the 50 Most Influential Minority Lawyers in America and by *Hispanic Business* magazine as one of the 100 Most Influential U.S. Hispanics in 2008. He is a three-time recipient of the Burton Award for Legal Achievement, most recently in 2011 for his article "Introducing Dodd-Frank," published in *Latin Lawyer.* In 2002, Galvis was part of a group of eminent practitioners

---

*Gacek participated in the Task Force under his previous affiliation with the American Federation of Labor and Congress of Industrial Organizations. As a current administration official, he has not been asked to join the Task Force consensus.

convened by a G10 working group to help develop collective action clauses for sovereign debt financings.

Kevin P. Green joined IBM in November 2004 and leads IBM's Department of Defense (DoD) and Intelligence Community business, which includes the U.S. Navy and Marine Corps, the U.S. Army, the U.S. Air Force, Joint Commands and DoD agencies, and National Security Intelligence agencies. Prior to joining IBM, Admiral Green spent thirty-three years as a naval officer, completing his navy career as deputy chief of naval operations (DCNO) for operations, plans, and policy. As DCNO, he coordinated global naval operations, strategic planning, information operations, and naval policy development and managed service relationships with the Office of the Secretary of Defense, the Joint Staff, the National Security Council staff, the U.S. military services, other federal agencies, and allied navies. As a flag officer, he commanded Naval Forces U.S. Southern Command, the *Abraham Lincoln* carrier battle group, and the Naval Training Center, Great Lakes, Illinois. He served in the Office of the Secretary of Defense, Atlantic Fleet headquarters, and the Bureau of Naval Personnel and commanded a destroyer squadron and a guided missile frigate. He graduated from the U.S. Naval Academy and the National War College and received an MS from the Naval Postgraduate School.

Donna J. Hrinak is vice president for global public policy at PepsiCo, Inc. She has served as U.S. ambassador to four countries—Brazil, Venezuela, Bolivia, and the Dominican Republic—and as deputy assistant secretary of state for Mexico and the Caribbean. She also had assignments in Colombia, Honduras, Mexico, and Poland. Ambassador Hrinak's honors include the U.S. government's Distinguished Public Service Award and the State Department's Career Achievement Award. In 2005, she was named international businesswoman of the year by the Miami chapter of the Organization of Women in International Trade. She serves on the board of directors of the Inter-American Dialogue and on the board of counselors of McLarty Associates. She is based in Purchase, NY.

Robert L. Hutchings is dean of the Lyndon B. Johnson School of Public Affairs at the University of Texas at Austin. Prior to this, Hutchings was diplomat in residence at the Woodrow Wilson School of Public and

International Affairs at Princeton University. He was also faculty chair of the master in public policy program and served for five years as assistant dean. From 2003 to 2005, on public service leave from Princeton, he was chairman of the U.S. National Intelligence Council. He has also served as a fellow and director of international studies at the Woodrow Wilson International Center for Scholars, as the National Security Council's director for European affairs, and as special adviser to the secretary of state, with the rank of ambassador. Ambassador Hutchings was deputy director of Radio Free Europe and on the faculty of the University of Virginia, and he has held adjunct appointments at the Johns Hopkins University School of Advanced International Studies and Georgetown University's School of Foreign Service. He is a director of the Atlantic Council of the United States and the Foundation for a Civil Society and is a member of the Council on Foreign Relations, the British-North American Committee, and the executive committee of the Association of Professional Schools of International Affairs.

G. John Ikenberry is the Albert G. Milbank professor of politics and international affairs at Princeton University in the Woodrow Wilson School. He has also taught previously at Georgetown University and the University of Pennsylvania. He has held posts at the State Department, on the policy planning staff, and at the Carnegie Endowment for International Peace, as a senior associate. Ikenberry has also been a nonresident senior fellow at the Brookings Institution. During 2002–2004, he was a transatlantic fellow at the German Marshall Fund. In 1998–99, Ikenberry was a fellow at the Woodrow Wilson International Center for Scholars. In 1997–98, he was a CFR international affairs fellow in Japan, sponsored by Hitachi Ltd., and spent a year affiliated with the Institute for International Policy Studies in Tokyo. He has published in all the major academic journals of international relations and written widely in policy journals in addition to authoring several books. He is also the reviewer of books on political and legal affairs for *Foreign Affairs*. Ikenberry has just published a new book, *Liberal Leviathan: The Origins, Crisis, and Transformation of the American World Order*. He received his PhD from the University of Chicago.

Timothy M. Kingston is a partner and managing director at Goldman, Sachs & Co., and coheads the global power effort within the investment banking division. He joined Goldman Sachs in May 1988, and his career has spanned various geographies and functional areas, including ten years in the Latin American group, where he served ultimately as chief operating officer and concentrated on Brazil. Kingston serves on the advisory boards of the Latin American studies program at Princeton University and the North American board of INSEAD and is a director of the North American Chilean Chamber of Commerce. He was previously a director of Mercado Libre. Kingston is a graduate of Princeton University and holds an MBA from INSEAD.

Thomas E. Lovejoy was elected university professor at George Mason University in March 2010. He also holds the biodiversity chair at the Heinz Center for Science, Economics, and the Environment and was president from 2002 to 2008. Starting in the 1970s, he helped bring attention to the issue of tropical deforestation, and in 1980, he published the first estimate of global extinction rates. Lovejoy has worked on the interaction between climate change and biodiversity for more than twenty years, coining the term *biological diversity* and originating the concept of debt-for-nature swaps. He is the founder of the public television series *Nature* and has served as the senior adviser to the president of the United Nations Foundation, the World Bank's chief biodiversity adviser and lead specialist for the environment for the Latin American region, the Smithsonian Institution's assistant secretary for environmental and external affairs, and executive vice president of World Wildlife Fund-U.S. He has served on advisory councils in the Reagan, George H.W. Bush, and Clinton administrations. In 2009 he was appointed conservation fellow by the National Geographic Society. He chairs the scientific and technical panel for the Global Environment Facility. He received his BS and PhD from Yale University.

Jennifer L. McCoy is director of the Carter Center's Americas program and has been professor of political science at Georgia State University since 1984. As part of her responsibilities overseeing the Americas program, she directs the Carter Center's Friends of the Inter-American Democratic Charter group, and she previously managed the Carter Center's project on mediation and monitoring in Venezuela from 2002 to 2004. She has directed election-monitoring missions for the Carter Center in Bolivia, Nicaragua, Panama, Mexico, Venezuela, Jamaica, and Peru and has participated in election delegations to Indonesia, Haiti, Suriname, and Guyana. McCoy's academic career has included extensive fieldwork in Venezuela, Nicaragua, and Uruguay, where she conducted research as a Fulbright fellow in 1991 and 1992. A specialist on democratization, international collective protection and promotion of democracy, and Latin American politics, McCoy's most recent book is *International Mediation in Venezuela* (with Francisco Diez). She is also editor and contributor to *The Unraveling of Representative Democracy in Venezuela* (with David Myers), *Do Politicians Learn from Political Crises?* and *Venezuelan Democracy Under Stress*.

Joy Olson is executive director of the Washington Office on Latin America (WOLA) and is a leading expert on human rights and U.S. policy toward Latin America. Under Olson's direction, WOLA is pioneering new approaches to human rights advocacy, focusing on the underlying causes of injustice, inequality, and violence. The *Washington Post* has recognized WOLA as one of the best-managed nonprofits in the Washington area. Olson specializes in military and security policy, and she has been a longtime advocate for greater transparency of military programs in Latin America. She cofounded the Just the Facts project, which makes information about U.S. military policy in Latin America publicly accessible. For more than a decade, she has coauthored an annual study on trends in U.S. security assistance, including the recent report *Waiting for Change*. Prior to joining WOLA, Olson directed the Latin America Working Group, a coalition of sixty nongovernmental organizations working to promote peaceful and just U.S. foreign policy toward Latin America. Olson has testified before Congress on Latin America policy issues ranging from human rights in Mexico to drug policy to the problems of poverty and inequality in the region. She is a frequent commentator in the media, including on CNN, CNN Español, the BBC, *PBS NewsHour*, National Public Radio, and an array of national and international news outlets. Olson earned an MA from the National Autonomous University of Mexico, following two years' work in community development in Honduras.

Brian D. O'Neill is vice chairman of Lazard International. His responsibilities include Latin America and Canada. O'Neill has extensive experience working with governments, local and multinational corporations, and financial institutions. He is a director of Signatura Lazard in Brazil and MBA Lazard in Central and South America and partner assigned to the firm's strategic alliance Alfaro, Davila y Rios S.C. in

Mexico. O'Neill served as deputy assistant secretary in the U.S. Treasury from 2007 to 2009. For a five-month period in 2008, he was acting U.S. director of the Inter-American Development Bank. Prior to that, he worked for JPMorgan Chase for over thirty years, where he held multiple leadership roles, including chairman of investment banking for Latin America and Canada from 2001 to 2006. He lived and worked in South America for twelve years in Santiago, Chile; Buenos Aires, Argentina; and São Paulo, Brazil. O'Neill is a director of the Council of the Americas, the Americas Society, and the Inter-American Dialogue. He is a member of the Council on Foreign Relations and a member of the advisory committee for the David Rockefeller Center for Latin America Studies at Harvard University.

Michelle Billig Patron is senior director of PIRA Energy Group. Prior to joining PIRA, Patron was an international affairs fellow at the Council on Foreign Relations and conducted energy research at Deutsche Bank. Earlier in her career, she served as an international policy adviser at the U.S. Department of Energy (DOE) under the Clinton and George W. Bush administrations. During that time, she advised the U.S. energy secretary and other senior U.S. officials on relations with major energy-producing and -consuming countries, including Venezuela, Mexico, Brazil, China, Nigeria, and the European Union. In 2001, Patron served as energy attaché at the U.S. Embassy in Beijing. Prior to the DOE, she worked at the International Energy Agency, the White House, UNICEF, and the Center for International Environmental Law. Patron holds a BA from Columbia University and an MA from the Johns Hopkins School of Advanced International Studies. She has served as a commentator to CNBC, BBC, NPR, the *New York Times*, and the *Economist* and has written for *Foreign Affairs*, the *Financial Times*, and the *Los Angeles Times*.

David Perez has served as a managing director with Palladium Equity Partners since 2003. Previously, he held senior private equity positions at General Atlantic Partners and Atlas Venture and also held positions at Chase Capital Partners and James D. Wolfensohn, Inc. Perez serves on the board of directors of Palladium's privately held portfolio companies Aconcagua Holdings, Inc.; American Gilsonite Company; Capital Contractors, Inc.; DolEx Dollar Express, Inc.; Jordan Healthcare Holdings, Inc.; and Prince Minerals, Inc. Perez serves as the chair of the board of directors of the National Association of Investment Companies, is a member of the Council on Foreign Relations, and is the president of the board of directors of Ballet Hispánico. Perez earned a BS/MS degree from the Dresden University of Technology, an MEng degree in engineering management from Cornell University, and an MBA from Harvard Business School.

Riordan Roett is the Sarita and Don Johnston professor of political science and director of Western Hemisphere studies at the Johns Hopkins Paul H. Nitze School of Advanced International Studies (SAIS). In 2004, SAIS announced the establishment of the Riordan Roett chair in Latin American studies. From 1983 to 1995, Roett served as a consultant to the Chase Manhattan Bank in various capacities; in 1994–95 he was the senior political analyst in the emerging markets division of the bank's international capital markets group. Roett is a member of the board of directors of several mutual funds at Legg Mason, Inc. He is a member of the Council on Foreign Relations and the Bretton Woods Committee and is a former national president of the Latin American Studies Association. He is author and editor of several books, including, most recently, *The New Brazil*. Roett received his BA, MA, and PhD from Columbia University.

David J. Rothkopf serves as president and chief executive of Garten Rothkopf. He is also a visiting scholar at the Carnegie Endowment for International Peace and chairs the Carnegie Economic Strategy Roundtable and the National Strategic Investment Dialogue. He is also the author of *Running the World: The Inside Story of the National Security Council* and *Superclass: The Global Power Elite and the World They Are Making*. His next book, *Power, Inc.: The Epic Rivalry Between Big Business and Government—and the Reckoning that Lies Ahead* will be published in 2012. He also writes a daily blog for ForeignPolicy.com. Prior to the establishment of Garten Rothkopf, he was chairman, CEO, and cofounder of Intellibridge Corporation, a leading provider of international analysis and open-source intelligence. Prior to that, he was managing director of Kissinger Associates, the international advisory firm founded and chaired by former U.S. secretary of state Henry A. Kissinger. Rothkopf served as acting U.S. undersecretary of commerce for international trade, directing the 2,400 employees of the International Trade Administration. He joined the Clinton administration in 1993 as deputy undersecretary of commerce for international trade policy development. Rothkopf was cofounder, chairman, and CEO of International Media Partners, Inc., publisher of *CEO* magazine and *Emerging Markets* and organizer of the CEO Institutes.

Andrew Small currently serves as the director of the committee that oversees relations between U.S. bishops and the Catholic Church in Latin America and the Caribbean. Father Small was the foreign policy adviser for the United States Conference of Catholic Bishops from 2004 to 2009. He has written extensively on the church's role in the public square and has delivered testimony before the U.S. Congress on the impact of U.S. trade policy on developing countries.

Julia E. Sweig is the Nelson and David Rockefeller senior fellow for Latin America studies, director for Latin America studies, and director of the Global Brazil initiative at the Council on Foreign Relations (CFR). She is the author of *Cuba: What Everyone Needs to Know* and *Friendly Fire: Losing Friends and Making Enemies in the Anti-American Century*, as well as of numerous publications on Latin America and American foreign policy. She has directed several CFR reports on Latin America. Sweig's *Inside the Cuban Revolution: Fidel Castro and the Urban Underground* received the American Historical Association's Herbert Feis Award for best book of the year by an independent scholar.

Tanisha N. Tingle-Smith is the principal and founder of Verdade Consulting, a boutique Brazil-focused risk advisory and research consultancy. Her research specializes in Brazilian international relations, with particular focus on the geoeconomics of Brazil's relations with the Global South. She has presented at and contributed to articles and book chapters for U.S. and international universities. In 2008–2009, she was a consultant at the United Nations Development Program on Brazil-Africa South-South development exchange. Earlier, she served as foreign policy analyst and adviser with the U.S. Central Intelligence Agency and the departments of State and Treasury. She received department recognition and awards for her analytic work. From 1995 to 2001, she was an analyst and assistant vice president for Latin America economic research with Salomon Smith Barney and Merrill Lynch. She is a term member of the Council on Foreign Relations. She holds an MIA from the School of International and Public Affairs at Columbia University.

James D. Wolfensohn is chairman of Wolfensohn & Company, LLC, chairman of Citigroup's international advisory board, and adviser to Citigroup's senior management on global strategy and on international matters. In 2006, he established the Wolfensohn Center for Development at the Brookings Institution. Wolfensohn was president of the World Bank Group from 1995 to 2005. He was special envoy for Gaza disengagement for the quartet of the Middle East; president and CEO of James D. Wolfensohn, Inc.; executive partner of Salomon Brothers, New York; executive deputy chairman and managing director of Schroders, London; president of J. Henry Schroders Banking Corporation, New York; and managing director of Darling & Co., Australia. He is chairman emeritus of the board of trustees of the John F. Kennedy Center for Performing Arts and of Carnegie Hall. In addition, he has been president of the International Federation of Multiple Sclerosis Societies, chairman of the board of the Institute for Advanced Study at Princeton University, director of the Business Council for Sustainable Development, chairman of the finance committee and a director of the Rockefeller Foundation and the Population Council, and a member of the board of Rockefeller University. He is an honorary trustee of the Brookings Institution, a member of the Council on Foreign Relations, and a member of the Century Association.

Task Force Observers

Fulton Armstrong
*U.S. Senate Committee
on Foreign Relations*

Daniel Kurtz-Phelan
U.S. Department of State

Elizabeth Lara
Wolfensohn & Company, LLC

Michael A. Levi
Council on Foreign Relations

Carl E. Meacham
*U.S. Senate Committee
on Foreign Relations*

Kellie Meiman Hock
McLarty Associates

Shannon K. O'Neil
Council on Foreign Relations

Peter A. Quilter
*U.S. House of Representatives
Committee on Foreign Affairs*

Matias Spektor
*Getulio Vargas Foundation
(Fundação Getulio Vargas)*

Jason Steinbaum
*House Subcommittee
on the Western Hemisphere*

Independent Task Force Reports

Published by the Council on Foreign Relations

U.S. Strategy for Pakistan and Afghanistan
Richard L. Armitage and Samuel R. Berger, Chairs; Daniel S. Markey, Project Director
Independent Task Force Report No. 65 (2010)

U.S. Policy Toward the Korean Peninsula
Charles L. Pritchard and John H. Tilelli Jr., Chairs; Scott A. Snyder, Project Director
Independent Task Force Report No. 64 (2010)

U.S. Immigration Policy
Jeb Bush and Thomas F. McLarty III, Chairs; Edward Alden, Project Director
Independent Task Force Report No. 63 (2009)

U.S. Nuclear Weapons Policy
William J. Perry and Brent Scowcroft, Chairs; Charles D. Ferguson, Project Director
Independent Task Force Report No. 62 (2009)

Confronting Climate Change: A Strategy for U.S. Foreign Policy
George E. Pataki and Thomas J. Vilsack, Chairs; Michael A. Levi, Project Director
Independent Task Force Report No. 61 (2008)

U.S.-Latin America Relations: A New Direction for a New Reality
Charlene Barshefsky and James T. Hill, Chairs; Shannon O'Neil, Project Director
Independent Task Force Report No. 60 (2008)

U.S.-China Relations: An Affirmative Agenda, A Responsible Course
Carla A. Hills and Dennis C. Blair, Chairs; Frank Sampson Jannuzi, Project Director
Independent Task Force Report No. 59 (2007)

National Security Consequences of U.S. Oil Dependency
John Deutch and James R. Schlesinger, Chairs; David G. Victor, Project Director
Independent Task Force Report No. 58 (2006)

Russia's Wrong Direction: What the United States Can and Should Do
John Edwards and Jack Kemp, Chairs; Stephen Sestanovich, Project Director
Independent Task Force Report No. 57 (2006)

More than Humanitarianism: A Strategic U.S. Approach Toward Africa
Anthony Lake and Christine Todd Whitman, Chairs; Princeton N. Lyman and J. Stephen
Morrison, Project Directors
Independent Task Force Report No. 56 (2006)

In the Wake of War: Improving Post-Conflict Capabilities
Samuel R. Berger and Brent Scowcroft, Chairs; William L. Nash, Project Director; Mona K. Sutphen, Deputy Director
Independent Task Force Report No. 55 (2005)

In Support of Arab Democracy: Why and How
Madeleine K. Albright and Vin Weber, Chairs; Steven A. Cook, Project Director
Independent Task Force Report No. 54 (2005)

Building a North American Community
John P. Manley, Pedro Aspe, and William F. Weld, Chairs; Thomas d'Aquino, Andrés Rozental, and Robert Pastor, Vice Chairs; Chappell H. Lawson, Project Director
Independent Task Force Report No. 53 (2005)

Iran: Time for a New Approach
Zbigniew Brzezinski and Robert M. Gates, Chairs; Suzanne Maloney, Project Director
Independent Task Force Report No. 52 (2004)

An Update on the Global Campaign Against Terrorist Financing
Maurice R. Greenberg, Chair; William F. Wechsler and Lee S. Wolosky, Project Directors
Independent Task Force Report No. 40B (Web-only release, 2004)

Renewing the Atlantic Partnership
Henry A. Kissinger and Lawrence H. Summers, Chairs; Charles A. Kupchan, Project Director
Independent Task Force Report No. 51 (2004)

Iraq: One Year After
Thomas R. Pickering and James R. Schlesinger, Chairs; Eric P. Schwartz, Project Consultant
Independent Task Force Report No. 43C (Web-only release, 2004)

Nonlethal Weapons and Capabilities
Paul X. Kelley and Graham Allison, Chairs; Richard L. Garwin, Project Director
Independent Task Force Report No. 50 (2004)

New Priorities in South Asia: U.S. Policy Toward India, Pakistan, and Afghanistan (Chairmen's Report)
Marshall Bouton, Nicholas Platt, and Frank G. Wisner, Chairs; Dennis Kux and Mahnaz Ispahani, Project Directors
Independent Task Force Report No. 49 (2003)
Cosponsored with the Asia Society

Finding America's Voice: A Strategy for Reinvigorating U.S. Public Diplomacy
Peter G. Peterson, Chair; Kathy Bloomgarden, Henry Grunwald, David E. Morey, and Shibley Telhami, Working Committee Chairs; Jennifer Sieg, Project Director; Sharon Herbstman, Project Coordinator
Independent Task Force Report No. 48 (2003)

Emergency Responders: Drastically Underfunded, Dangerously Unprepared
Warren B. Rudman, Chair; Richard A. Clarke, Senior Adviser; Jamie F. Metzl, Project Director
Independent Task Force Report No. 47 (2003)

Iraq: The Day After (Chairs' Update)
Thomas R. Pickering and James R. Schlesinger, Chairs; Eric P. Schwartz, Project Director
Independent Task Force Report No. 43B (Web-only release, 2003)

Burma: Time for Change
Mathea Falco, Chair
Independent Task Force Report No. 46 (2003)

Afghanistan: Are We Losing the Peace?
Marshall Bouton, Nicholas Platt, and Frank G. Wisner, Chairs; Dennis Kux and Mahnaz
Ispahani, Project Directors
Chairman's Report of an Independent Task Force (2003)
Cosponsored with the Asia Society

Meeting the North Korean Nuclear Challenge
Morton I. Abramowitz and James T. Laney, Chairs; Eric Heginbotham, Project Director
Independent Task Force Report No. 45 (2003)

Chinese Military Power
Harold Brown, Chair; Joseph W. Prueher, Vice Chair; Adam Segal, Project Director
Independent Task Force Report No. 44 (2003)

Iraq: The Day After
Thomas R. Pickering and James R. Schlesinger, Chairs; Eric P. Schwartz, Project Director
Independent Task Force Report No. 43 (2003)

Threats to Democracy: Prevention and Response
Madeleine K. Albright and Bronislaw Geremek, Chairs; Morton H. Halperin, Director;
Elizabeth Frawley Bagley, Associate Director
Independent Task Force Report No. 42 (2002)

America—Still Unprepared, Still in Danger
Gary Hart and Warren B. Rudman, Chairs; Stephen E. Flynn, Project Director
Independent Task Force Report No. 41 (2002)

Terrorist Financing
Maurice R. Greenberg, Chair; William F. Wechsler and Lee S. Wolosky, Project Directors
Independent Task Force Report No. 40 (2002)

Enhancing U.S. Leadership at the United Nations
David Dreier and Lee H. Hamilton, Chairs; Lee Feinstein and Adrian Karatnycky, Project
Directors
Independent Task Force Report No. 39 (2002)
Cosponsored with Freedom House

Improving the U.S. Public Diplomacy Campaign in the War Against Terrorism
Carla A. Hills and Richard C. Holbrooke, Chairs; Charles G. Boyd, Project Director
Independent Task Force Report No. 38 (Web-only release, 2001)

Building Support for More Open Trade
Kenneth M. Duberstein and Robert E. Rubin, Chairs; Timothy F. Geithner, Project Director; Daniel R. Lucich, Deputy Project Director
Independent Task Force Report No. 37 (2001)

Beginning the Journey: China, the United States, and the WTO
Robert D. Hormats, Chair; Elizabeth Economy and Kevin Nealer, Project Directors
Independent Task Force Report No. 36 (2001)

Strategic Energy Policy Update
Edward L. Morse, Chair; Amy Myers Jaffe, Project Director
Independent Task Force Report No. 33B (2001)
Cosponsored with the James A. Baker III Institute for Public Policy of Rice University

Testing North Korea: The Next Stage in U.S. and ROK Policy
Morton I. Abramowitz and James T. Laney, Chairs; Robert A. Manning, Project Director
Independent Task Force Report No. 35 (2001)

The United States and Southeast Asia: A Policy Agenda for the New Administration
J. Robert Kerrey, Chair; Robert A. Manning, Project Director
Independent Task Force Report No. 34 (2001)

Strategic Energy Policy: Challenges for the 21st Century
Edward L. Morse, Chair; Amy Myers Jaffe, Project Director
Independent Task Force Report No. 33 (2001)
Cosponsored with the James A. Baker III Institute for Public Policy of Rice University

A Letter to the President and a Memorandum on U.S. Policy Toward Brazil
Stephen Robert, Chair; Kenneth Maxwell, Project Director
Independent Task Force Report No. 32 (2001)

State Department Reform
Frank C. Carlucci, Chair; Ian J. Brzezinski, Project Coordinator
Independent Task Force Report No. 31 (2001)
Cosponsored with the Center for Strategic and International Studies

U.S.-Cuban Relations in the 21st Century: A Follow-on Report
Bernard W. Aronson and William D. Rogers, Chairs; Julia Sweig and Walter Mead, Project
Directors
Independent Task Force Report No. 30 (2000)

Toward Greater Peace and Security in Colombia: Forging a Constructive U.S. Policy
Bob Graham and Brent Scowcroft, Chairs; Michael Shifter, Project Director
Independent Task Force Report No. 29 (2000)
Cosponsored with the Inter-American Dialogue

Future Directions for U.S. Economic Policy Toward Japan
Laura D'Andrea Tyson, Chair; M. Diana Helweg Newton, Project Director
Independent Task Force Report No. 28 (2000)

First Steps Toward a Constructive U.S. Policy in Colombia
Bob Graham and Brent Scowcroft, Chairs; Michael Shifter, Project Director
Interim Report (2000)
Cosponsored with the Inter-American Dialogue

Promoting Sustainable Economies in the Balkans
Steven Rattner, Chair; Michael B.G. Froman, Project Director
Independent Task Force Report No. 27 (2000)

Non-Lethal Technologies: Progress and Prospects
Richard L. Garwin, Chair; W. Montague Winfield, Project Director
Independent Task Force Report No. 26 (1999)

Safeguarding Prosperity in a Global Financial System:
The Future International Financial Architecture
Carla A. Hills and Peter G. Peterson, Chairs; Morris Goldstein, Project Director
Independent Task Force Report No. 25 (1999)
Cosponsored with the International Institute for Economics

U.S. Policy Toward North Korea: Next Steps
Morton I. Abramowitz and James T. Laney, Chairs; Michael J. Green, Project Director
Independent Task Force Report No. 24 (1999)

Reconstructing the Balkans
Morton I. Abramowitz and Albert Fishlow, Chairs; Charles A. Kupchan, Project Director
Independent Task Force Report No. 23 (Web-only release, 1999)

Strengthening Palestinian Public Institutions
Michel Rocard, Chair; Henry Siegman, Project Director; Yezid Sayigh and Khalil Shikaki,
Principal Authors
Independent Task Force Report No. 22 (1999)

U.S. Policy Toward Northeastern Europe
Zbigniew Brzezinski, Chair; F. Stephen Larrabee, Project Director
Independent Task Force Report No. 21 (1999)

The Future of Transatlantic Relations
Robert D. Blackwill, Chair and Project Director
Independent Task Force Report No. 20 (1999)

U.S.-Cuban Relations in the 21st Century
Bernard W. Aronson and William D. Rogers, Chairs; Walter Russell Mead, Project Director
Independent Task Force Report No. 19 (1999)

After the Tests: U.S. Policy Toward India and Pakistan
Richard N. Haass and Morton H. Halperin, Chairs
Independent Task Force Report No. 18 (1998)
Cosponsored with the Brookings Institution

Managing Change on the Korean Peninsula
Morton I. Abramowitz and James T. Laney, Chairs; Michael J. Green, Project Director
Independent Task Force Report No. 17 (1998)

Promoting U.S. Economic Relations with Africa
Peggy Dulany and Frank Savage, Chairs; Salih Booker, Project Director
Independent Task Force Report No. 16 (1998)

U.S. Middle East Policy and the Peace Process
Henry Siegman, Project Coordinator
Independent Task Force Report No. 15 (1997)

Differentiated Containment: U.S. Policy Toward Iran and Iraq
Zbigniew Brzezinski and Brent Scowcroft, Chairs; Richard W. Murphy, Project Director
Independent Task Force Report No. 14 (1997)

Russia, Its Neighbors, and an Enlarging NATO
Richard G. Lugar, Chair; Victoria Nuland, Project Director
Independent Task Force Report No. 13 (1997)

Rethinking International Drug Control: New Directions for U.S. Policy
Mathea Falco, Chair
Independent Task Force Report No. 12 (1997)

Financing America's Leadership: Protecting American Interests and Promoting American Values
Mickey Edwards and Stephen J. Solarz, Chairs; Morton H. Halperin, Lawrence J. Korb,
and Richard M. Moose, Project Directors
Independent Task Force Report No. 11 (1997)
Cosponsored with the Brookings Institution

A New U.S. Policy Toward India and Pakistan
Richard N. Haass, Chair; Gideon Rose, Project Director
Independent Task Force Report No. 10 (1997)

Arms Control and the U.S.-Russian Relationship
Robert D. Blackwill, Chair and Author; Keith W. Dayton, Project Director
Independent Task Force Report No. 9 (1996)
Cosponsored with the Nixon Center for Peace and Freedom

American National Interest and the United Nations
George Soros, Chair
Independent Task Force Report No. 8 (1996)

Making Intelligence Smarter: The Future of U.S. Intelligence
Maurice R. Greenberg, Chair; Richard N. Haass, Project Director
Independent Task Force Report No. 7 (1996)

Lessons of the Mexican Peso Crisis
John C. Whitehead, Chair; Marie-Josée Kravis, Project Director
Independent Task Force Report No. 6 (1996)

Managing the Taiwan Issue: Key Is Better U.S. Relations with China
Stephen Friedman, Chair; Elizabeth Economy, Project Director
Independent Task Force Report No. 5 (1995)

Non-Lethal Technologies: Military Options and Implications
Malcolm H. Wiener, Chair
Independent Task Force Report No. 4 (1995)

Should NATO Expand?
Harold Brown, Chair; Charles A. Kupchan, Project Director
Independent Task Force Report No. 3 (1995)

Success or Sellout? The U.S.-North Korean Nuclear Accord
Kyung Won Kim and Nicholas Platt, Chairs; Richard N. Haass, Project Director
Independent Task Force Report No. 2 (1995)
Cosponsored with the Seoul Forum for International Affairs

Nuclear Proliferation: Confronting the New Challenges
Stephen J. Hadley, Chair; Mitchell B. Reiss, Project Director
Independent Task Force Report No. 1 (1995)

To purchase a printed copy, call the Brookings Institution Press: 800.537.5487.
Note: Task Force reports are available for download from CFR's website, www.cfr.org.
For more information, email publications@cfr.org.